MORE
ANSWERS

THE HILARION SERIES

THE NATURE OF REALITY: Scientific and occult riddles explained. Ends with prophetic section on the apocalypse. Updated version available in Fall of 1985.

SEASONS OF THE SPIRIT: A journey into man's unrecorded history. Many insights into palmistry and other esoteric areas.

SYMBOLS: Explains the signs, portents and allegories of earth life.

ASTROLOGY PLUS: The planets in signs and houses, seen esoterically. A rich mine of new information on the science of the stars.

THRESHOLD: Simply written introduction to Hilarion material.

NATIONS: Karma, lessons and destiny of 25 earth nations.

OTHER KINGDOMS: Fascinating encounters with other beings and life-forms, mostly unseen, which interact with man on earth.

DARK ROBES, DARK BROTHERS: Expose of the methods and purpose of the entities that oppose man's spiritual progress.

BODY SIGNS: The symbolic meaning of the organs and systems of the body. Includes a complete course on esoteric palmistry.

WILDFLOWERS: Spiritual uses of 25 common wayside plants.

VISION: Rebuilding civilization in a spiritual mold.

ANSWERS and **MORE ANSWERS:** Two books which together reproduce all of the responses made to questions submitted by subscribers to the newsletter, Lightline, from 1980 to 1982.

TAPESTRY: A magnificent overview of our life-stream, its progress through the eons of its pilgrimage, and the future vistas.

THE SCARLET CASTLE: A tale of adventure and fantasy based on the Hilarion approach to life. A treat for young and old alike.

EINSTEIN DOESN'T WORK HERE ANYMORE: M.B.Cooke develops the Hilarion scientific concepts from first principles. Contains directions for generating inert gas beams.

OTHER AUTHORS

A NEW HEAVEN, A NEW EARTH: by Seven Rays. This channeled book discusses the challenge of restructuring society and humanity on Aquarian principles.

Write for a complete listing of these books and other items.

INTRODUCTION

Many readers of the Hilarion Series of books will be aware that, during the early 1980's, we published a regular bi-monthly newsletter called *Lightline,* in which questions submitted by subscribers were answered through the telepathic channel that I have developed. For a number of reasons, the publication of that newsletter was halted in 1982. Since that time we have been inundated with requests for back issues from people who were not aware of the Hilarion material while the newsletter was available. To answer this demand, Marcus Books has already published about half of all the *Lightline* commentaries in a book called *Answers,* appearing in 1983. The present book contains the rest of the material, specifically the answers appearing in *Lightlines* 1 through 5, 6/7, 13, 14, 15, 19 and 20/21.

The only commentaries omitted from this text are the summaries of the Universal Laws which appeared in *Lightline* 20/21. These discussions have already been incorporated in our book, *Vision,* and need not be repeated here.

For readers curious about the nature of the channel through which this material has come, I suggest a reading of the introduction to our book, *Other Kingdoms.* There they will find a good summary of the approach which this source takes to earth-experience, viewing it always against the great panorama of transcendant realities which make up the created cosmos.

It is my hope that the material in this book will strike a resonant chord in many people who are searching for a broader viewpoint from which to assess their own reality. And I am happy to know that these interesting commentaries will now be preserved permanently.

Maurice B.Cooke
Toronto, Canada
February, 1985

CONTENTS – INDEX

Due to the nature of this book, a standard Table of Contents is not feasible. There are no chapters or sections to identify. The material consists of about 114 commentaries in question-and-answer format. Because the questions are not grouped as to subject matter, it is felt that the most useful 'contents' would be an alphabetical index of the topics dealt with. That follows:

General Message to LIGHTLINE Readers:

We are very pleased that yet another channel for light has come into being. We have deliberately attempted to promote this publication in the minds of its originators, in order that we could have a clear and current channel for reaching those who are attuned to the energies of the New Age. In future editions, we hope to be able to provide a better grasp of the nature of events in the earth than could normally be obtained from conventional sources. In doing so, we expect to be able to influence many souls to put their energies to work in bringing about the outflowering of love and light and spirituality which lie at the core of the New Age.

Only when man sees with his own eyes the stark evidence of the wrongness of his ways will he be prompted to change *himself*. And only when this *inner* change is accomplished will the human family be able to walk together into the New Age of peace, brotherhood, enlightenment and love.

Can you discuss the purpose and role of sadgurus (realized beings) in the scheme of things? How does one know for sure that they are divine beings?

This is a complex question to answer. There are many levels of attainment among those who walk the earth in this age. Some are of little development, and are drawn only to that which is base and unworthy. Others, though tempted and drawn off the path by the world's attractions, retain an inner knowledge of their goal and their purpose. Still others have, in past incarnations, succeeded in raising their vibrations to the point required to escape from the wheel of rebirth and the karmic necessity. Yet they have voluntarily taken on physical bodies so that they could be of service to their brothers, as teachers, helpers, healers etc. In this last category fall many of the Gurus and Masters which have allowed themselves to come into the public eye. However, *not all* of those who permit others to revere them as advanced souls have in fact reached this status. These are intended to tempt the unwary seeker, so that he (the seeker) may learn to sharpen his discernment in the future, and not again be led astray. The best test for anyone to apply to such Gurus is that of the "inner voice". If your own inner voice tells you that this or that person is right for you to follow or to listen to, then do it. But ensure that your reasons for following him are not tainted. Do not do it because it is a fad, or because your friends believe, or because others of his followers have befriended you. Do not do it for *self*, but for *truth*. A final word of warning, however, is in order. There is a law that the true master never proclaims that he is such. His followers may think as they please, but he never does or says anything which gives others to believe that he considers himself an advanced soul. Any Guru or "Master" who proclaims that he is such or who endeavors to make you think that he is more spiritually advanced than you, is definitely nothing of the sort.

Could you please give a definition of what you mean when you use the word "karma"?

The question which has been asked about karma has largely assumed karma to be negative karma, that is, karma which results from actions taken which were against the Creator's Laws. (Most people think of karma in this way). This is the reason why we have also taken the same point of view in our books. More broadly, however, karma simply means the law of cause and effect, and where the actions taken by an individual are nurturing and supportive of others, so the karma which is accumulated is of the same vibration, and comes back to lighten the life and the lives which that individual will be living subsequently. Turning to the negative kind of karma, we may explain by saying that every action which a human being undertakes is in a sense, always with that individual as if it were adhered to him. As such, if these actions were negative, if they resulted in pain or distress to another creature of any kind, they act as a literal hindrance for the harming soul, for it is literally a burden which the soul carries about. In order to cut away from the soul that negative or dark complex which resulted from the action, it is necessary normally for the soul to pass through an equivalent episode of pain or difficulty. If that can be brought about in the same life or a subsequent one, then the negative karmic consequences of the original act can be removed.

What has been the effect of the Mt. St. Helens eruptions on Eastern Canada, both physically and spiritually?

The effects have been enormous. Firstly at the physical level, the eruptions have allowed large quantities of baser substances to fill the atmosphere over all of Canada, and much of the rest of the world. These materials are without exception of a kind tending to interfere with the normal energy patterns in the human body. This is a difficult process to explain in your language, but it may be looked on as 'dust' or 'grit' which adheres to the nerves and other pathways of the body, limiting the free flow of signals which those paths are intended to carry. These paths include those which are active in acupuncture and those which are stimulated in foot and hand reflexology.

At the spiritual level, there is a precise parallel which was given as an allegory for those who have eyes to see. This relates to the name of the lake which was, for a period of time, blocked up by mud slides from the mountain volcano. The lake was called "Spirit Lake", and this was meant to symbolize, for those who are able to read the symbols around them, that the major effect of the eruption of the volcano, in the sense of the higher levels, was that the access which the *spirit* or *soul* was able to have with the earth personality was blocked or stopped up, at least to a degree.

Are there any particular life lessons to be learned through the asthmatic condition? Can it be alleviated?

The physical affliction known as asthma is a karmic flow in the aetheric body which from time to time interferes with the physical breathing apparatus. The trigger for the asthma attack can be emotional, or it can be due to particles of a certain kind in the air. However, the nature of the triggering influence has little directly to do with what is being learned by the asthmatic through undergoing this condition.

Asthma derives from *misuse of energy.* There are many souls who have been given access to considerable power and energy in past incarnations, but who have misused it for personal gain, or to bring pain to others. Whenever this occurs, an automatic flaw in the aetheric pattern for the body arises, and this brings the weakness about. Thus, through the operation of this automatic process, the victim of asthma is deprived from time to time of access to air (oxygen), and without this access he is rendered weak and sometimes totally incapacitated. This condition is meant to remind him, at the level of his higher self, that he yet must work out the problem of the right use of energy. Also, of course, the deprivation of energy is the karmic repayment for having misused energy in the past.

Is the pendulum an acceptable device for everyone?

Yes, the pendulum, properly used and understood, is an

excellent method for virtually anyone in incarnation to obtain information and advice not normally available to the conscious mind.

Is there any way of using the pendulum which will avoid unconsciously affecting the outcome?

The nature of the question suggests that the process at work in using the pendulum has not been understood. Reference is made to "unconsciously affecting" the outcome. And yet the *unconscious* is *precisely* that which is first contacted by anyone who uses the pendulum method. The pendulum is, first and foremost, a method by which any individual in incarnation can obtain access to the vast memory stores and the knowledge that has been implanted in the unconscious. Now, having said that, we must elaborate by pointing out that in almost every case of pendulum use, there is an access of some sort to sources which go beyond the person's own unconscious.

Let us explain the process by stages. When you first take up the pendulum channel and work with it, you are initially placing yourself into contact with your own unconscious. However, each soul in incarnation has a guide and perhaps one or more "teachers" who are eager to offer help to the seeking soul by any means, including the pendulum. Now, as the individual becomes more adept at using the pendulum, the teachers and the guides also learn how to influence the pendulum answer for those questions which go beyond the contained knowledge in the unconscious. Hence, whenever the pendulum is asked something which the unconscious does not know, the other entities will try to answer. It is in this way that a "channel" can be built-up, i.e. a channel to something more than merely the individual's own unconscious. Indeed, this process of experience and build-up is precisely how the present channel was developed. After enough "matching" had taken place between this source and the minds (both conscious and unconscious) of the individual who is the channel, permission was given for the channel to be converted from a pendulum channel to a verbal one.

Technically, what is the best way to operate the pendulum?

This varies from person to person, but generally a technique as follows will be found to work quite satisfactorily. Obtain a key, ring or the like of similar weight, and tie it to the end of a string at least a foot long. Place the elbow of the writing arm on a table while seated, with the forearm extending forwardly and upwardly at about a 45 degree slope. With the hand, grasp the end of the string and allow the key to hang down to a point just above the table top. On a piece of paper draw a cross, labelling one cross-arm "yes" at both ends, and the other cross-arm "no" at both ends. It does not matter which is which. Now, simply hang the key, etc. over the crossing point of the two arms, "release" the arm mentally, do not try either to hold it still or to move it, and then concentrate on the question you wish to have answered.

At first it is better to state the question out loud, in order to alert the unconscious to the fact that it is being asked something. Sometimes the question must be repeated several times before the answer will come. This is normal at first. Also, it must be realized that the unconscious must "learn" how to manipulate the forearm through the triggering of tiny impulses in the arm before it can confidently answer any question. We recommend that at least one week be taken up with simple exercises to allow the unconscious to become familiar with the technique. Thus, you may practice by asking the unconscious to swing "no", and then to swing "yes" and then to swing on an angle between them, etc. Next start with obvious questions: "Am I a man?", "Am I married?", etc. After your *unconscious* has learned how to manipulate the pendulum without hesitation, *and only then*, will your guides or teachers attempt to add additional input to your conscious mind through the pendulum.

Can you discuss the mantram "OM MANI PADME HUM" which you use at the end of each of your books?

The phrase is a Holy Breath from the highest possible source. We are aware that many will not understand what we mean by Holy Breath, but perhaps we can explain by saying that, at the level from which this dictation is originating, there are inputs of spirituality and light from yet higher planes, in exactly the same way that channels of this kind, scriptures, and way-showers represent inputs of higher spirituality for your own level. One of the ways in which a higher input comes to this level is in the form of a Holy Breath. There are locations in this particular level where any soul or entity can "go" in order to be overshadowed by these still higher sources of light and purity. The impulse which is experienced comes as a "breathing" which we term "Holy Breath" (the closest English equivalent).

Now, the expression Om Mani Padme Hum is the sound-equivalent in an ancient earth language of one of the main patterns of energy which comes as a Holy Breath to us at this level. In that ancient earth language, it means "Honor to the jewel in the Lotus". But the phrase also has meaning in the Angel Tongue, which men once knew but have forgotten. The meaning in the Angel Tongue is this: *"There is the One and there are the Many. The mystery of the One is that it has become the Many. The destiny of the Many is that they must return to the One."*

This idea sums up the entirety of the manifestation of separate fragments or God-sparks, its purpose and its ultimate aim. It was allowed into the world as a reminder to the souls of men that the pilgrimage on which they are embarked is part of the vast plan of God Himself as He strives towards self-realization.

7

Do our souls have a primary sex even though we all experience both sexes in the course of numerous lifetimes?

The soul of the average individual does lean toward one sexual role more than the other, as a rule, but this 'leaning' is much less marked than in the case of an incarnated personality.

Can children's programs on television have a detrimental effect on toddlers and small children?

There is no question but that the main effect of any television program on any individual, whether child or adult, is detrimental. There are a few exceptions, in which the content in spiritual terms compensates for the physical, astral and aetheric jangling which takes place during the watching of the television tube's picture, but such high quality programs are rare. They are mostly those in which classical music is played as a background or as the main focus of the program.

Dealing firstly with the physical effect, this is always negative due to the strain on the eyes and the nervous system from watching an image which is not constant. Because the image is traced by running points of light which cross the screen many times each second, the brain must blend these fragments together into a single picture and this causes undue strain. Using the senses to focus on anything which is not natural is always a source of stress.

Secondly, the astral level of the watcher is normally adversely affected by the *content* of most T.V. programs available today. This content is typically one filled with conflict, violence, or the exhibition of emotions (sadness, grief, self-pity, etc.) which drag the quality of the astral vibrations down. The only emotion which ennobles the astral is that of love, friendship, affection. Anything not of this vibration is a detriment.

Third, the aetheric body is very adversely affected by the

8

radiation which is given off by the apparatus itself, particularly from the screen surface. The electrical interplay taking place produces vibrations in the aether which jangle the aetheric body and throw off the finely tuned pathways of energy transfer which are essential to its proper functioning.

Finally, we wish to turn to the content of certain so-called educational programs, especially for children. There is only one way to teach a small child, and that is while it is immersed in an environment of love, acceptance and encouragement. Humour or stimulating visual images or rapid change *do not* make learning easier. They merely lead to an addiction to this stimulation, which keeps the child watching. There is of course some value in terms of using repetition, for example the alphabet or numbers, but the amount of good that can be accomplished by this repetition is far overshadowed by the harmful effects which we have discussed above, and the addictive tendencies of most North American T.V. "styles".

Please explain the more untoward effects of smoking on the physical body. Is there anything that can ease the quitting process? Are there any predispositions in some physical vehicles towards smoking? Are there any conditions under which smoking is warranted?

The most negative effect of smoking is of course in the lungs of the person addicted to this unfortunate habit. These become coated with a layer of carbon deposits which the body cannot rid itself of readily. It requires up to nine months of no smoking whatever before most physical bodies are able to dislodge the last of the deposits, and even this short time requires fasting and much purification of other intakes — especially food. Flowing from the coating on the lungs is an interference with the body's ability to make full use of the prana in the oxygen of the air. This prana is the real energy source of the body, and interference with the assimilation of this wondrous material is *always* negative for the individual, since it limits the clarity of thought, the stamina of the body, and the warmth of the affections.

There is little that we can recommend through this channel with regard to the quitting process. There are certain herbs which some individuals find helpful, but they do not work for all. In the last analysis, there must be a *decision* to quit. The difficulty which most "quitters" have is related to the fact that they are not *fully* committed to quitting. There is a remaining desire in many cases to have the pleasure of the inhalation of smoke and until this desire for the pleasure can be overcome, the likelihood of success is small.

This leads to a point which we consider important to make. In regard to all habits which *stimulate* the physical body — like smoking, coffee, rich foods, drugs and over-indulgence in sex — there is a process at work which will shed much light on the nature of the relationship between the higher and lower selves. Consider the average person today in incarnation. He is bombarded with temptations to direct his attention solely to the earth plane, to indulge himself in all the pleasures which the earth makes available, and to pay no heed to the plight of his fellow beings. All of these activities place *distance* between him and his higher self or soul. The knowledge and wisdom of the soul has difficulty in gaining access to the conscious mind of the incarnated individual. Because of this distance, the feeling of wholeness and completeness which is the birthright of every human is absent to a greater or lesser degree. In order to make up for this lack, many individuals resort to stimulants of the kind we have listed above, because this gives them temporarily a feeling which is something like what would always be theirs if their higher and lower selves were in close communication.

But these very habits — coffee, smoking, drugs and the like — pollute the physical vehicle in a way which makes it *even harder* for the more intimate contact to come about. It is therefore a vicious circle in which they have become entrapped. The more they smoke, for example, the greater is the difficulty in contacting the higher self. This leads to a stronger desire to smoke in order to have the stimulation, which leads to more smoking, more distance, and so forth.

We should point out that there are some individuals who can retain an awareness of the higher truths and a contact with their higher selves, despite a smoking or coffee habit. These "drugs" are minor compared with aspirins, barbiturates and the other strong substances. However, in every case the awareness and higher contact could be improved by halting the smoking habit.

It should also be pointed out that some individuals are of such a nervous disposition that without something in the mouth or held in the fingers (both locations being very strong focal points for nerve energy), the nervous structure would be unduly strained. What we are saying here is that for these people, it is not the smoke in the lungs that is of benefit (since it obstructs contact with the higher self in every case), but rather the holding of the cigarette in the hand or mouth. Thus there are a few instances in which retaining the smoking habit is apparently the lesser of two evils, as it were.

What is the effect on a nonsmoking individual of being in the presence of a smoker?

It is essentially the same as for the smoker, so long as there is some smoke passing into the lungs. However, the interference with prana assimilation is a matter or degree of smoke inhalation. The less smoke in the lungs, the less the problem. There are *psychological* factors which affect non-smokers in the presence of smokers, however. These factors are often related to a tendency for non-smokers to identify smoking with undesirable activity generally, or with that which is unspiritual. In a sense, smoking does symbolize that which is dark or evil, even though many who smoke are themselves quite spiritual. It is simply the *symbol* of the smoke itself: the unconscious associates this with destruction, loss, and evil.

Is the wearing of synthetic fabrics in any way detrimental to the physical vehicle?

The wearing of any garment at all is an interference with the natural energy pathways in the physical, astral and aetheric bodies of man. However, it is not to be expected that society could be quickly converted to the view that clothes wearing is something that should be avoided. In any event, in northern latitudes the wearing of some covering for warmth is quite essential in the present phase of man's experience upon this planet.

In certain past societies, a conscious or unconscious recognition of the fact first stated led to the development of garments which had the least detrimental effect on the various bodies of man. In certain portions of the Roman experience, for example, extremely lightweight togas and robes were in fashion, and these were able to cover the body to the extent demanded by modesty without greatly interfering with the energy flows we have spoken of. Rome however was centered in a warm climate, and clothes were not needed so much for warmth.

Turning to the specific question that has been asked, we can say that, if clothes must be worn, the natural fibres tend to be better from the aspect of not interfering with the *physical* energy patterns to a great degree. However, both kinds of fabric do cause some interference.

We should point out that the worst possible kind of garment, from all points of view, is leather. Leather comes from the body of an animal that has been killed by man, and all who wear such clothing take on some of the karma related to that death. The karma is slight, however, compared to the damage done to the individual by the thought-form of fear and desperation which clings to every

12

leather garment. This also includes furs, or course. The negative effect is considerably less when the article is smaller, for example a leather belt or leather shoes. Nonethe less the detriment is still present.

If the destiny of the race is to rise to higher levels of conscious awareness and vibration, is this not in conflict with the idea of man entering the "core of the earth", and thus penetrating deeper into matter (i.e. the earth itself)?

This question arises from remarks which we have made in the first of our books, *The Nature of Reality*. We wish to point out to you that that particular book was written in a very special way, for it had a particular purpose and function to perform. It was intended to take away the walls of skepticism and unbelief and narrowness which surround so many human beings on the earth in these days. As a result, the book was written in a particularly mantramistic and stark form. If you will re-read certain passages with an understanding of what the word "mantramistic" means you will understand that what we were attempting to do was reach through the conscious mind to higher levels, without the person really willing to allow it to happen, in order to bring about a brightening of the Inner Light. Because the Inner Light is so encrusted with walls of atheism, skepticism, doubt, and self-interest, it is sometimes necessary to be almost brutal in one's attempt to accomplish what will ultimately be for the soul's own good and evolution. Now, with reference to the concept of the centre core of the earth . . . this is a much misunderstood idea. There is a Truth behind what we have said in *The Nature of Reality*, but it is a more complex picture than we were able to paint in the book. There are many levels of vibration on the earth which interpenetrate and which are not simply broken down into physical, astral, and aetheric. You are familiar with the tales of the little folk, the fairies, the leprechauns, and so forth which many have claimed to have seen. These entities and creatures are able to exist and pass into and out of certain higher states of vibration which allow them to either be seen or not, at their choosing, by humans who remain in the base or lowest state.

The centre core area of the earth pertains mainly to this higher state and can only be entered in that state. It is possible to go there, but not if you remain at your base level of vibration. Now the concept that the centre core of the earth is the only rescue location for mankind is oversimplified. Yet we did not feel that it would be of advantage to explain the great complexity of the overall operation of rescue. Thus the question which you have asked is not fully appropriate to the broader perspective which we have tried to show you. Certainly it is true that mankind is intended to rise to ever higher levels of vibration, evolution, love and light. But the temporary sojourn inside the earth is not a retrograde step in that sense. Indeed, the souls who actually live lives in that area in the other vibration are generally of a higher level of evolution than those on the surface. It is a question, in a sense, of *proximity* to the centre point of light in the Earth's own body. One can only exist in close proximity to this centre source if one's own vibrations are also raised.

Do those born under the astrological sign of Aquarius carry a special purpose, benefit or karma, in view of the coming "Age of Aquarius"?

The aquarians by sun-sign are those who are *generally* in tune with the principles of the new age — i.e. affection between groups and individuals, and the technical side of development. However, aside from this deep attunement (which may not be fully manifesting due to filters and overlays which they have taken on in the incarnational process) such persons are no more or no less than their brothers. Each person has his own karma, his own special lessons still requiring effort, and his own path in spiritual terms.

To what extent can we expect physical damage to Toronto (and the general area), during the coming upheavals?

The question requires us to extrapolate present tendencies into the future. We must point out to you that, even though the general course of this chaotic period has been outlined and will be followed, nonetheless the future for any specific location is not set, for it is dependent largely upon the vibrational level of the human beings who inhabit it. We have pointed out (ref. the book *Symbols,* ed.) that the Toronto area, and generally the Southern Ontario area is a location in which souls who incarnate are largely of an evolved nature. They are, for the most part, born into situations in which they are not encouraged to see the Truth of the Spirit. Nonetheless, they have within them an intuitive knowledge of this Truth and when the right promptings and events are witnessed it is the hope that this awareness will awaken in them and that they will no longer be blind. Because of the nature of the souls who have incarnated in this general area it is expected that their own vibrations will, by the operation of inflexible higher laws, act to protect them and the area (for so long as they remain in it) from the worst which is set to befall the earth. We say that as long as they inhabit the area the area will be protected, but you are all aware that there are plans to remove large numbers of human beings from the path of danger when the threat reaches its worst point. We do not wish to dwell on the nature of this operation of rescue for it has many facets. However, we can assure you that so long as your purpose and resolve remain fixed to the highest spiritual good then your own personal environment can only be that of protection and Light.

Would you please comment on the subject of Ley-lines?

15

The concept of ley lines upon the Earth's body can be compared to the concept of meridians in acupuncture. The Earth has a body, as does Man, and upon this body are marked certain communication lines along which spiritual or higher level energies can flow. It is the fact that there are many more acupuncture meridians in the physical body or more accurately in the astral counterpart than are presently recognized. The major lines are understood, just as in the etheric body the major chakras are recognized, but in the astral there are an almost endless number of minor or smaller channels of energy transfer which pass between various subsidiary focuses of this energy, and likewise at the higher or etheric level, there are almost numberless minor focuses of etheric energy throughout the body. Similarly, with the Earth, there are major ley lines and there are minor ley lines; there are also numerous points where these cross at what may be termed nodes, and at these nodes the amount of energy available from the Earth itself is increased. In many of the large cities of the Earth you have at least two, and sometimes three, crossing energy paths with important nodes being situated in the cities. In a sense, it is this energy which has drawn the Family of Man to these locations in order to set up the civilized centres where he can live.

What is the Anti-Christ? Can we expect a person to embody the anti-christ?

The earth plane is the plane where all things must manifest as opposites, as two sides or poles. There cannot be light without dark. There cannot be the positive without the negative. Man must be balanced by woman; and so forth. The great teacher and the saving force for mankind on this planet is the Christ. We refer not just to the manifestation of the Christ when it lived with the man Jesus in Galilee, but to the eternal principle of *Christ Love* which permeates and enlivens all of manifestation — indeed which literally lives at the heart of all that is made. But, in order to allow this Christ force access to the plane of matter, there had to be a simultaneous manifestation of its opposite, which has been called the Anti-Christ.

The Anti-Christ is not a person. It is a *principle*. It has been allowed to influence many individuals who have lived on the earth plane, and so in a sense such persons can be looked on as overshadowed by the Anti-Christ force. Such figures as Attila and Hitler are obvious, but in more recent times there have been those who have manifested certain facets of the Anti-Christ — in politics, in business, and in the military. One has only to think of the history of the past few decades in order to hit upon a dozen or more such "anti-christs".

The question is whether one can expect that a specific person will manifest as the Anti-Christ. Our reply is that many represent that principle now. But it is up to the discernment of each individual as to whether he will be able to detect those who are overshadowed in this way.

Message: First published in the Atlantean Era.

This is a time for all of those who have remained aware that there is more to life than is apparent at first glance to unite in thought and in heart for the salvation of the human race and the experiment which it represents. This is a call not only to those in incarnation upon the earth plane, but also to those working from other planes and levels and who wish to see the Plan for humanity unfold as it was intended to.

In the next few years, a great change will be imposed upon this planet. It will be a stepping up of all vibrancy levels affecting the various life-forms on earth, including man. Those who have remained aware of the higher truths and the meaning and purpose behind existence will be able to absorb the new energies flooding into the earth much more easily than those whose focus has been turned to lower and less worthy concerns. All who have given themselves over to selfishness, anger or violence, or who are trapped in the snares of materialism, will find the new energies extremely difficult to assimilate, and as a result they will see the patterns of their lives very much disrupted.

In parts of the world where the less evolved souls have been allowed to incarnate — we refer to countries in Asia and Africa as well as parts of eastern Europe and South America — the conflict between the new energies and the average vibration of individuals will produce far more upheaval and disruption than in the more soul-advanced regions of the earth. Nonetheless, the human family is *one* and the trials of any part affect the whole. For this reason, the disruptive events over the next few years — the war, the hunger, the political and economic instabilities — will inevitably have repercussions in *all* countries of the world. The widespread chaos that will result represents the acting out of the prophetic visions of the Apostle John as related in the Revelations, and it will culminate finally in what Christian Scriptures call the Battle of Armageddon — a last coming together of all the armies of the world in the land surrounding Jerusalem, there to obliterate each other in an outpouring of human rage and blood thirst that will have had no equal in all the eons of time since man was placed upon this planet.

In some writings, this time of trouble leading to the Apocalypse is referred to as the Tribulation, which is the term we have used in our own books. Regardless of the name applied, it is certain that none who experience this great trial will never forget the test which they underwent. That memory will be a spur to perfection and soul evolvement whose effect will be so strong that the other galactic races — who have all along doubted whether man on this planet could ever succeed in his quest for spiritual light — will be amazed at how quickly the human race learns the spiritual way of living, and even surpasses many of *them* in terms of allowing the principle of love to guide civilization's progress.

We are grateful for this opportunity to address readers of this publication, and wish to assure all that our thoughts, our love and our strength are ever available to those in incarnation, if they but open themselves to the higher vibrations being flooded constantly into the earth. Now is the time for the rescue and uplift of the human race, and any who wish to be a part of the great work of salvation now in progress may count on our help.

May the peace and blessing of all the higher beings who care for humanity's struggle be with you forevermore.

OM MANI PADME HUM

Hilarion

Please comment on the significance of the entire hostage crisis. What can we learn in symbolic terms from the fact that the hostages were released on their 444th day, just when the 40th president of the U.S. took office?

It is evident that the person framing this question has grasped the nature of the numerological portents which surrrounded the double event of the release and the inauguration. The number four is of course the number which best identifies the earth plane, its limitations, shortages, rivalry and incitement to warfare. It is the number which characterizes those who "rub others the wrong way", who have a chip on their shoulder, and who find that conflict and resentment are their daily lot in life. This is not, of course, anything which is being imposed upon such individuals from outside. On the contrary, these persons are simply experiencing in the reality of their lives the manifestation of the states of being which are within themselves. In all such persons — all those who meet continually with conflict in their lives — there is a deep well of resentment against their brothers. This festering pool of hatred has been nurtured through many lives, and no great effort

19

has ever been made to overcome the tendency toward rivalry and aggression. Thus, the traits of violence and resentment become ever more ingrained into the soul.

We have diverged from the direct question in order to cast some light on the basic numerology represented by the four. Now to turn to the specific focus of this question, it is true that something important was being signalled by the convergence of all the fours on the very day when the 40th president of the United States was being inaugurated. Indeed, the numerology extends even further. If one adds all the numbers in the inauguration date, one has 1 (Jan.) $+ 2 + 0 + 1 + 9 + 8 + 1 = 22$, and $2 + 2 = 4$.

The basic message hidden in the numbers surrounding this double event was that the meanings normally attached to the four will be found to characterize the presidency: that is, warfare, aggression, limitations, shortages.

At what point in the Tribulation will Jesus Christ appear? Will the Christ who reappears be able to manifest himself to man at many locations simultaneously?

The man who was Jesus will appear to his faithful brothers at different times, depending upon when each individual achieves those qualities of soul that are prerequisite. The qualities are simple: a loving heart, a desire for truth, and the absence of negative emotion. This is the secret not only of the awareness which allows the other planes to become visible, but also of maintaining abundant good health for many decades beyond what is now considered the normal lifespan.

What we are saying is this: Jesus lives always in the hearts of His human brothers. If any would look into the secret places of his own heart, and ask Him to show Himself, then He would certainly make His presence known. This may not always be visibly, and it is not expected that all will sense His presence in terms of bodily form. But many will do so, as their third eye begins to open. Indeed, there are those now on the earth who have already walked and talked with the Master, for they have been given the gift of the higher sight.

From the occult point of view, what is the significance of the entry of Uranus into Sagittarius? (February 17 to March 20, 1981; and beginning November 16, 1981 for seven years).

The significance is different, depending upon the level of meaning you are looking for. From the most advanced plane of viewing, the significance is summed up in the word, *Revelation.* It is a time for the revelation of new truths and new concepts on the earth plane. These new ideas will come from higher planes and flood downwardly into the consciousness of man, since all truly spiritualizing force proceeds from above.

From the next point of view, that of the practical level of consideration, the meaning is that of *fulfillment of prophecy.* During the seven years of Uranus' sojourn in the sign of the Seer, there will come to pass many of the patterns foreshadowed in various prophecies which man has been given in the past, especially those found in the Christian Scriptures.

Finally, for those whose personal life-patterns are strongly influenced by the sign of Sagittarius, the significance is that of *change* and the sudden blossoming of new and previously hidden facets of life and experience. For many under the influence of Sagittarius this will entail moving into a life pattern that is quite unexpected, one which they had not thought would be theirs in this incarnation.

Is the thinking of Hal Lindsey on the Rapture consistent with your own?

There is a perfect consistency except for a few minor

points.

The following unabridged material is taken from the complete transcript of a question-and-answer session with "Bob and Jane" for their Toronto Star column (Nov. 23/ 80).
Why do whales beach themselves?

Yes, we are aware of these tragedies. The whale species is not what it seems. We have written in our books that these magnificent kings of the sea are in reality ensouled by entities of very high status, who have wished to make their vibrations manifest on the earth plane, to benefit all creatures — especially man but also those in the sea. There has been in recent times so much negativity and conflict in the very atmosphere of the earth, that it has caused these magnificent creatures (we speak of the higher part of the creatures) to lose heart in the endeavor which they were making. They have decided that they can serve better from a higher plane, and therefore they have caused the physical vehicles which they were enlivening to be done away with in a most tragic form. It is difficult for us to speak of this sad act, because at this level we feel more deeply than you could know when any major tragedy or loss occurs on the earth plane.

Do we understand the correct meaning of astrological houses? If not, what should be the interpretation?

Generally, the nature and interpretation of the houses of a birth chart are well understood by astrological practitioners. The only comment we should make is that the division of the intermediate houses would be more accurate if done by the Porphery system, provided the rising point is correct. This system trisects the celestial arc in each quadrant of the chart.

Are contraceptive methods such as the pill, the I.U.D. and prophylactics harmful to the body? From a spiritual level is there anything negative or karmic in practising birth control?

This question should be discussed first from the higher point of view, because the approach in the spiritual sense will automatically answer the queries at the more earthly level.

The act of giving birth to the vehicle of another soul is among the greatest gifts one human being can offer to another. At the same time, the earth plane itself is arranged so that it can support only so many individuals of the human family at a time. Hence there must be some control over the numbers of incarnated souls on the planet at any given point. Prior to the present, the control always came about through the natural processes of disease and famine, and the total number of souls on the planet never before approached the "limit number" of 5 billion. This figure represents the maximum for the human life form on the planet, and cannot be exceeded without dire consequences for the body of the earth itself. This limitation does not arise through exhaustion of food sources or oxygen, as might be thought. There is enough land area on earth to support a hundred times the limit number, if all were vegetarians as man was meant to be. Instead, the limit comes about at the aetheric level: The mental "presence" of humanity *en masse* is very powerful, and this power tends to be proportional to the population. If the earth population were to exceed 5 billion, the power of man's thought would exceed the power of the earth logos itself, and thus an imbalance would result. It is not possible for us to explain this difficulty more clearly, as the concepts required have no words in earth language.

We have digressed from the original question in order to

explain a little of the background behind the question of population control. Turning to the spiritual implications of birth control, then, we can state that to decline to provide a channel for the entry of another soul into incarnation is not an act which generates karma or any negative results of a similar kind. It is simply a decision made by each individual and is within the right of the individual to make.

However, the only sure way to avoid becoming such a channel is to avoid intercourse entirely. The reason for this is as follows. The act of sexual intercourse is one which sets up considerable energies between the lovers — energies that seek to manifest in the form of pregnancy and birth. These energies have a great deal of power and it is very often necessary for the guides of an individual to intervene in order to prevent conception when the life circumstances are not appropriate. This is true even where intercourse took place on a so-called "safe" day. In reality there are no "safe" days. The ability of the energies we have described to keep sperm alive and viable for several days, or to bring about the discharge of an ovum at a date off the normal schedule, is remarkable. Many people who have studied spiritual matters and who understand the general functions of the guardians have the idea that it is *they* who manipulate and arrange pregnancy, whereas in fact these guardians usually (as we have said) intervene to *prevent* it.

Now, whenever an individual attempts to "block" the body's natural tendency to become a channel for birth, as prompted by the powerful energies we have described, various difficulties — of greater or lesser seriousness — arise. Where the prevention is strictly mechanical, for example placing a diaphragm or sheath in the normal path of the sperm seeking the ovum, the consequences are confined to the aetheric and higher levels. As we have explained in our book, *Seasons of the Spirit,* the act of sexual intercourse is intended to allow the partners to interchange root chakra energy, in order to balance up or complete the lack in each person of energies characteristic of the other.

Thus, the man receives female energies, while the woman

24

receives male energies. When the act of intercourse is accompanied by a full sharing of this kind, a sense of great relaxation and at-one-ment results. However, the imposition of any mechanical barrier which prevents or substantially prevents the tissues from directly contacting each other will act to greatly *reduce* this interchange of male-female energies. The result will be a residue of continuing sexual tension in one or both partners, and a feeling that the experience was not fully satisfying. This can build up over a period of time, and ultimately manifest in other areas of the relationship.

If the means of preventing pregnancy involves drugs or chemicals, there will arise a great conflict between the channelling energies which we described earlier and the strictly earth-level forces released by the drugs. These latter are essentially material only, and thus represent "dead" processes, without life in them. By contrast the energies seeking to become a channel for birth are very alive and powerful. The conflict which results almost always has deleterious effects on the body of the person taking the drugs (usually the woman). The effects are often to alter the nature of the blood to increase clotting tendencies, thus causing more pain in menstruating. Often, headaches and other general symptoms are also found to accompany the taking of the pill to avoid pregnancy.

As to the karmic implications of mechanical or chemical methods of birth control, such are confined to the simple cause-and-effect mechanisms we have already described. There is no karma carried over by the higher self to another life, because the effects of the method of birth control are always manifested in the same life in which it is practiced, and usually simultaneously with the method.

It is not necessary to comment at length on the I.U.D., since the same general principles apply. These mechanical devices implanted in the womb do a great deal of damage to the energy flow-paths from the root chakra, and as a result, lower abdominal complications almost always are met with, if not during the time that the device is in place, then somewhat later in the same life pattern.

Finally, there is the matter of surgically cutting either the fallopian tubes or the equivalent passages in the male. As we have pointed out in a previous answer, the severing of these important passageways disrupts the flow of root chakra energy to the lower abdomen, and near-term or long-term physical deterioration is almost always the ultimate result.

Again, the karma is simply the very results we have described at the physical level.

It is said that there is someone for everyone. Is this true? If so, how might I contact him/her?

There is indeed a mated soul for each person in incarnation. However, it is rare that the soul-mates are allowed to be on the earth plane together. The reason for this general prohibition is that, if such were to happen, and if the mates located each other, then they would become so focused on each other and the near perfection of their relationship, that they would cease to strive to overcome their flaws and short-comings.

Since the earth plane is the place where the most can be done the quickest in terms of improvement, it would not do to waste the experience of a life just drifting in a blissful relationship with the soul-mate.

In addition to the specific mated soul, of course, there are many other souls with whom a great bond exists. These make up the so-called "soul family". For most of the souls in one's own family, one will feel a deep bond of affection, unless certain filters (astrological, etc.) stand in the way. When that happens, it is hoped that the souls will strive to overcome the contrary filters, and will learn to allow the true affection to flower.

Many laboratories use test kits containing radioactive

material. Are these low-level exposures (about one milli-curie) harmful or dangerous to the body?

This is a complex question. The complexity arises because the levels of radioactivity that are damaging to one body may be quite harmless, or even beneficial, to another. Essentially it is a matter of purity of the body itself. Those physical vehicles which have been abused through many years of improper diet and negative thought are more likely to be harmed by radioactivity. Conversely, those whose vehicles have been purified are able to utilize the energies of the radioactivity in a positive way.

We should remind all that the sort of change which comes about in cell nuclei as a result of radioactivity is responsible for mutation, and that without mutation, no spontaneous advance in the genetic sense is possible. Indeed, it is expected that the relatively high levels of radiation on the earth which result from the forthcoming nuclear war will have opposite effects depending upon the vibration of the persons subjected to them. If the victim of radiation exposure is of low vibration and has a body incapable of transforming these energies into positive factors, then the radiation may initiate the disintegration of key tissues and ultimately lead to death. On the other hand, a person who has purified his physical vehicle and has attuned himself with the positive energies of the New Age will find that exposure to the same level of radiation will bring about positive transmutations within himself, for example the opening up of higher gifts such as that of aetheric sight. We are not saying that a person on the Path should go out and expose himself to radiation in an attempt to force occult gifts into the open. He would run a great risk that the level would be too high. It is best simply to await events, knowing that those entities who have humanity in their care have planned the coming phase in great detail, and that all who are intended to be transmuted through radiation will be exposed to just the right dose, without having to be concerned with what that dose is.

What happens when people commit suicide? Do they go into a state of limbo?

The question of suicide is a complex one. Generally speaking, the suicide is taking his own life in order to end the pain of existence — or at least what *he* perceives as pain. Usually this is emotional or mental pain, rather than physical. When the life is cast away for such a selfish reason, the law requires that the post-life experiences be somewhat more limited than is usually the case, and generally, the soul will be allowed less option in determining the nature and circumstances of the next incarnation. Also, there is an unavoidable requirement for the soul that has taken its own life while in incarnation, to be presented with precisely the same test in the next life — i.e. the same temptation to commit suicide. In the next life, that temptation will be even stronger, and the forces impelling him to take his own life will be even more difficult to resist. At the same time, the incarnated personality who must endure this harder test will also be given more "weapons" with which to fight the temptation, which usually means being on the receiving end of more love and support during the childhood phase.

The idea that such souls go into a kind of limbo has some validity, but it must be realized that *always* such limbo experiences are of the personality's own making. The experience of being in a "fog" without anything substantial around one arises simply from the *expectation* of the individual that, after death, there will be *nothing*. Since the astral realms always conform themselves to the mental expectations, the person will be presented with exactly what he expects: *nothing*. In time, since the individual is in his astral body — which he can feel — he will ultimately realize that he must in fact be existing. When this happens, he can be contacted by rescuers who specialize in such work, and can be coaxed out of his self-imposed fog or limbo. If only the person had realized before death that he would survive the killing of the body, such a limbo state would not arise. And in all probability, the person would not have taken his own life. Most suicides believe that death is the end of consciousness, and it is this "obliteration" which they are seeking in their desperate act.

Can you explain the difference between saying OM (pronounced like "home") and AUM?

The sounds which the human voice can make are marvellous in their occult properties. There are sounds which can calm the storm, others which can recall a departing soul to the physical form, others which can literally command the spirits of demons to do one's bidding. However, these words of power have been denied to man ever since he lost his ability to discern the correct use of the gifts in his possession. It was observed that, when he was given metal, he made spears and swords; when he was given fire, he made explosives and used them to kill, when he was given the power of articulating sounds, he formed words that could hurt and wound. So it was decided that humanity could not be entrusted with these mighty sounds of power. Only one man in the past age has fully been given these words, and that was Jesus. This He merited because of the purity which He embodied.

Turning to the specific question, we can explain that both of the sounds referred to are lesser examples of vibrations capable of summoning only positive energies. It was decided to permit such sounds and words, because they are not capable of negative use.

Essentially, the sound OM is the closest human-speech equivalent to the sound of creation itself. By making that sound, the human being aligns and attunes himself with the creative forces at many levels. The sound AUM, however, is the literal name of a specific entity which is in a position of guardianship with respect to the human family. By uttering his name, the speaker requests that this entity come into the speaker's vibration, and give whatever help may be needed.

Please comment on the role of Anwar Sadat as a peace-maker in the Middle East. Will he have a role in the New Age? (Answered prior to his assassination)

This beautiful soul has volunteered to live a sacrifice life in order to demonstrate to the peoples of the Moslem faith that constant hatred and warfare can be overcome, and that the way to overcome them in the outside manifestation is firstly to expunge them from within oneself. The soul of Sadat is one of great light and purity. This can be seen in his face. Likewise, the faces of other leaders in the middle east also truly reflect their real essence.
We are not permitted to say what lies in store for Anwar Sadat.

Please comment on the process of pregnancy and birth. Why is there such a degree of discomfort and pain felt by many women?

The process of birthing another soul is one of the most beautiful and meaningful experiences that a human in incarnation can possibly have. It was never intended to be accompanied by the least amount of pain or discomfort. The pain and difficulty which many experience arises through several causes. The first is of course the expectation that there *will* be pain in giving birth. This sets up a subconscious blockage against accepting the birth experience, and when the labour contractions begin, the subconscious attitude tries to resist the opening of the cervix by literally holding it shut. This produces a conflict between the natural process of opening the cervix to allow the new soul to enter the world, and the subconscious desire to delay or arrest the process.
The second cause of discomfort in childbirth relates to the

faulty diet which most women in the western countries follow. This diet reduces the capacity of the tissues to stretch and dilate, as the cervix must do in order to allow the foetus into the birth canal.

The final important cause of labor and birthing pain is the matter-of-fact approach which society generally has to the whole idea of having a baby. It is not seen in the light in which it should be viewed, namely as one of the most wonderful and holy of all possible human experiences, for it is literally the act of creating a new temple for a soul to inhabit. While it is true that the soul who is about to come into the world also contributes importantly to the creation of the foetus, nonetheless the mother must also give much of herself in the process, and undergo considerable restrictions, as well as providing the nourishment for the new life inside her. If mankind could view the birthing process in the proper spirit of reverence and wonder, then the mother-to-be would not find her own excitement in conflict with the average attitude, and this at-one-ment would ease the process still further.

Although childbirth was not intended to be painful in any way, the guides of humanity do utilize the pain that is felt (due to the above causes) to allow karma to be set aside. What better way to atone for having taken a life in a past experience than to be the literal channel through which that soul is given life again? Moreover, the pain that is felt can be used to discharge karma that arose at the time of taking another's life. The entities who guide humanity's progress realized that in childbirth lay the ideal way to allow souls to offset karma from having ended the life of another, without requiring the perpetrator to lose his own life.

Many religions promote the idea of mourning the dead. Is grief the right way to react to the death of someone close?

The clinging to one who has departed the earth, regardless

of the circumstances of his passing, can only bring pain to the person who insists on looking backwards in this manner. More importantly, the soul of the deceased is actually held back in its progress by any untoward or magnified grief or yearning. The best thing that anyone can do for an individual that has made the transition is to let him go, to wish him well, to pray for his rapid progress and to turn the attention toward the *future*. Grief is an extremely selfish emotion. The one who mourns is mourning for *himself*, is pitying himself for being now left alone. This is not love or loyalty, and it is certainly not helping the one who has passed over. If there was indeed any real love felt for the deceased individual by the one surviving him, the way to show it is to beam that love toward him, to pray for his rapid progress, and then to *let go*. Only in this way can happiness eventually come to the survivor, and only in this way can the deceased get on with his path of learning and progress.

If meat-eating is not for human beings as God intended, why would He place the inuit peoples in the far north where no food other than meat is available for survival?

First, it is not *God* Who has placed the Inuit in the far north. The souls of these native people have chosen to incarnate under those harsh conditions for very special reasons. One of the reasons relates to the general explanation as to why certain souls are drawn to northern climes while others are attracted to the south. It is essentially a question of like attracting like, for those who are drawn to colder climates are those whose *emotionalism* is subdued and, in a sense, 'cooler' than that of others. Conversely, the souls who incarnate into warmer countries are those whose emotional impulses are less under control. Think of the aloofness of the British, as compared to the volatility of the Italians. In a sense, the "thought-form" of the country or region itself has a filtering effect upon the souls who incarnate there, so that one incarnating in England would tend to "pick up" a certain reserve from the vibrations of that country, even if he had not quite that degree of aloofness himself at the higher level. However, this thought-form is itself the result of the thoughts of the millions of souls making up the country, and so to some extent one has the chicken and egg problem. Nonetheless, we think the above makes the process of country-selection more clear.

Turning to the second reason why the Eskimo and other groups incarnate into the far north, this lies in the fact that such souls have wished to atone for and set aside karma of a very serious nature arising from a previous life in which they exhibited a heartless attitude toward others, i.e. treated others *coldly*. By *themselves* being treated "coldly" by the very climate into which they incarnate, much of the burden that lies upon them can be discharged. If, at the same time, they incarnate along with a group of souls who are such that little compassion or tenderness will be shown by any of them toward any other, then a second manner of meeting the karma is available. Finally, by being born into a culture which is forced to eat the meat of animals that must be individually killed by the hunter with his own hands or weapons, these souls are being forced to live through echo-experiences harking back to the lives when the original karma was set up – lives in which they dealt with human beings as they are now dealing with the animal life around them. This, it is hoped, will remind them of the original acts, at least on a subconscious plane. In this manner they can make a connection between the life-pattern which they are now experiencing – with all its harshness and difficulty – and the initial actions which resulted in the necessity for the present life in the far north.

From the foregoing it can be seen that the necessity to be born in the far north where the only food is meat has a meaning far beyond the question of the propriety of consuming animal flesh. Indeed, the problems and the karma with which these souls are wrestling are much more serious than the simple matter of meat-eating. In a sense, until these individuals learn to have compassion for other human souls, they can never be expected to expand that compassionate point of view to the extent of embracing all of the life-forms on the planet. Indeed, their very lack of compassion for other forms is one of the reasons why they are now living in a region where the *number* of other life-forms is very limited. If any should doubt our assertion regarding the lack of warmth and compassion, they need only read of the traditions which such people have developed, traditions in which family members who are no longer useful to the community are allowed to die in the cold.

The following is a transcript of a reading given after a Christmas Group Meditation in December, 1979.

We wish to greet all of you on this holy occasion of the year; we have been following your deliberations and meditations with great interest and we have of course participated from our side in what you have been doing. It is appropriate to take a minute now and explain to you the importance of the meditative work you are doing as *we* see the importance.

Meditation has many abundant advantages from *your* point of view in terms of connecting you with your higher self and the bringing through of higher energies from the upper planes. However, from our point of view, the great importance of a meditation group is that it allows us to flood the earth with positive energies of the kind which will be greatly needed in the dark years ahead. The energies of love and light are the most in need now in the earth and it is on occasions like this, particularly at this time of year, that this service is possible for us to render to the earth and to our earth brothers. We send to you our thoughts and our love and our strength; these are always available to you to tap into if you but go into the silence of meditation as you have been doing.

Meditation

Meditation, as with many earthly activities and those that are not so earthly, is a highly individual matter. It is not appropriate for us to give one hard and fast routine or explanation which would be suitable for all souls in incarnation. The nature of the meditation experience for each soul is as different as the souls are different from each other. However, we can explain some of the categories of meditative experience which certain people will find that they have, in the hopes that it may allow you to recognize the category you have appeared to be experiencing.

Firstly, when you go into the silence, which is the term we use for meditation, your guides and guardians utilize the opportunity which is presented, to offer more in terms of explanation, spiritual insight and love wisdom, than is normally available to the conscious mind. This information is brought to you in pictures, allegories, feelings, sounds and so on, which are impressed upon the mind when it is in the meditative condition. For this experience to take place, it is not necessary to rise up to a higher level, for the guides and guardians try to send the love wisdom down to you. Indeed, by so doing they send additional energy which passes into the earth plane at the same time you pick it up, which means that merely by the meditative act, you are helping your brothers without needing to concentrate on sending the energy elsewhere. This leads to the *second* category.

Many souls in incarnation, among this group in any event, are capable of acting as what we might call transformers of energy; that is, the energy which is passed down from higher planes is run through a particular soul in incarnation, and, in passing through that particular soul, it is transformed to a different vibration. We hesitate to use the word "lower", because it is not made lower in the sense of worse or poorer, merely that it is changed to a vibration that is accesible to your brothers who still grope in darkness and there are many millions of them. When this experience happens, in which energy is felt to be building up within the body, it is simply a matter of allowing the energy to flow through, rather than damming it up; thus the energy will flow out abundantly into the earth plane. It is not always the experience that the same soul will have the energy feeling each time. In one meditative experience we may choose one individual and at other times another to act as a primary transformer.

The *third* category is one in which the mental body is taken elsewhere and allowed to see the actual form of the created worlds. This, for the novice, is sometimes difficult to distinguish from the purely allegorical or symbolic pictures which are impressed upon the mind. With practice, you will get to the point where you can distinguish actual travel experiences from experiences of being shown pictures or holographs.

The final category is the effect of actually beaming energy to specific recipients who may be in need of it. For example, requesting that the energy be sent to those who are weaker is an excellent exercise. By merely holding in your mind a picture of the person you wish to receive the energy, the energy automatically flows; you do not have to do much beyond simply visualizing the face or essence of the person to whom you wish to channel the positive, healing energies.

You have asked the best direction to focus thoughts at this time to help humanity . . . we can do no better than to urge all to continue on in the direction you are going... each of you should follow his own heart, his own inner voice.

The Iran Situation . . . How can we contribute?

The best contribution you can make is either prayer or meditation, depending upon what you are most comfortable with. Visualization would be used in imagining that the present impasse will be resolved and that the hostages will be freed. You simply imagine that it has already taken place: not that it *will* but that it has *already* taken place. That is the strongest kind of thoughtform. It is much more likely to bring about the reality which it contains.

A general comment on the situation: It is certainly possible that the present impasse will lead to the final war. Indeed, we see it as a contributing factor, but the future is not set, even at this date. The specific ways in which the final conflagration will erupt are not absolutely set. One thing apparently clear, however, is that the difficulties between Iran and the U.S. are serving to polarize the two factions into unified camps and these camps will find themselves at odds with each other over the oil question within the near future.

Canada's involvement in the possible war

At this time there are two forms of energy being flooded into the world . . . the negative energy which is being added to those human beings who are basically attuned to lower vibrations, and at the same time positive energies are being flooded through those like yourselves who are attuned to the higher vibrations. This is necessary in order to keep the world stable. There must not be too great a preponderance of one or the other because the nature of the human race is not such as to allow itself to absorb only the one or only the other and remain stable. This will come in the future when the vibration of the entire race is raised and the median kind of energy can go up accordingly; but right now, there must be energies on both sides of the median. Those human beings that are attuned to the lower vibration are allowing these lower or darker vibrations through and it is these darker energies that are inexorably leading to the disintegration of the world system as these people see it. However, from the point of view of those not tied to the materialistic concerns, egotism, selfishness or pleasure, the disintegration of the system built upon these concepts will not be seen as a catastrophe, but rather as a great step forward . . . as if the entire Universe were opening up like a beautiful flower.

Therefore, those who are on the positive side of the light will see the Universe unfold beautifully before them, and will see the fruits of their endeavours to help their brothers, whereas those whose attention is directed downwardly into the earth, into materialism, selfishness and so forth, will be aghast at the destruction and disintegration which they see around them. This process will be unvarying and will continue right through the entire period of chaos which is coming, whether or not Canada is involved in the final war . . . it certainly will be, though this is some time off for the North American continent. For other countries it is sooner. However, we can tell you with our whole heart that those who are working for the light and for the spirit will be completely and utterly protected from all negative influences in terms of that conflagration.

It is extremely warming and gratifying to those of us who have been expending so much energy in the same direction that you are moving, to see that your efforts are beginning to bear fruit . . . if we can bring others into circles of this kind . . . encourage all to work as hard as possible for the victory of light over darkness . . . then the years of chaos will rest less heavily upon the planet and much can be salvaged of what you now see about you. Work hard for this goal and it will be achieved.

Housing — its influence on the spiritual development of Man . . .

The matter of the most appropriate environment for the human being in terms of his spiritual, mental and emotional development is a complex one. You are aware that human beings are of many different vibrations, which may be considered in a broad way to fall into seven categories.

In the case of each category it is possible to say that a different kind of living environment is the most appropriate one. We refer here to shape, texture, colour and so forth.

Now, let us explain firstly that the shape in which man has primarily been living for most of his development period has been perfectly related to the moral, spiritual, mental and physical condition that he has had to the present time. You are aware that most of the buildings inhabited by men, particularly in terms of residential housing, have involved a rectangular or squarish lower section, and a triangular or three-pointed upper section forming a peak at the top. In terms seen from higher up, this has been a perfect representation on the one hand of the material, practical and separative nature of physical existence as it is lived in practical terms on the earth, and on the other hand of the higher aspirations and the spiritual striving of the human heart and soul. The lower portion, being the square, stands also normally as a four-cornered geometric figure on the earth. This corresponds with the number four (ref.p.10 *Seasons of the Spirit*) which is the number that correlates with the separative, rivalrous and contending nature of man's life on the earth, where he must fight for the ownership of property, goods and so forth . . . this is the meaning of the number four and this is why it has been quite natural for man to divide up his property into four-cornered pieces and to build his houses and buildings basically as four-cornered structures.

But, above and beyond the practical, materialistic and earth-centered consciousness of the lower self, stands the higher self, or eternal soul. It is this portion of man that knows the great truth that man is not just a physical being, but consists of three basic facets: the mental, emotional and physical. Indeed the matter is much more complex than this and continues to the higher self, which also embodies three facets corresponding at a much higher level to the mental, emotional and physical. The triangle is taken as the eternal and, if you like, general symbol of the higher knowledge, the truths of the spirit, the great light and glory of the soul which exists in and above each man.

Thus, the roof with its peak and its triangular shape represents one facet of the human being, the lower portion of the house with its square, rectangular shape represents another. When you sum the four and three together you have the number seven which pertains to the higher aspirations of the race, the worlds beyond, the attainment of the loftiest peaks on the mountain of spiritual achievement: this being the pilgrimage that each human being has embarked upon. At the same time, you could simply take the shape, i.e. the square at the bottom and the triangle at the top, and ignore the intermediate lines to count five points in all, five lines or edges, to the figure. It becomes an irregular pentagon which represents the perfect balance which mankind was intended to strike between the number *one*, representing God the Unmanifest, and the number *nine*, representing God the Manifest. There are many levels to this discussion and it is not necessary to deal further with all details at this point. You have asked what are the best materials, shapes, configurations and colours. Man in his heart knows the best for him, for even though the square and rectangular figures have been associated with the practical rivalry and difficult part of man's history, that in which he contended with his own brothers for ownership, at the same time the right-angle of the figure, i.e. the fact that the walls run perpendicular to the ground, is also a very *high* symbol which was intended to show that there is a "right" way, that there is the idea of standing upright before God, that the soul has a correct path before it if it wishes to take it; Man speaks of "the straight path", or the "straight and narrow". The "straightness" and the idea of perpendicularity are symbols which are reminding man that it is indeed the task of his soul while it is in incarnation to seek the straight and narrow, to stand upright before God. This is also why attempts to introduce among mankind other shapes which depart from the standard shape of the square base and the triangle at the top have failed, generally, to appeal to broad masses of men. It is expected that, as the consciousness of the race increases in vibration, as it rises to the next level in its evolution, there will be found more and more the circular or dome-like shape. This has already been introduced to some extent into the world by Buckminster Fuller and others who have come from a very high level of civilization in other areas of the created universe, as you might already suspect, and who have brought their knowledge of what is appropriate at these much more advanced levels to their earth cousins. But we do not see at the present time a broad acceptance of these newer ideas. What perhaps might be needed is an improvement of the basic, already accepted forms. You are aware of the beautiful feeling of spiritual expansion that one feels when entering a Gothic church, or any building with high ceilings. This is because it allows, literally, the spiritual part of the human being, related to various extensions of the aura, to rise up to the full extent of the space in which the human being is located. That is very important, and it is an unfortunate thing that humanity, thinking to make the best use of the available space, has built buildings with very low ceilings. These literally oppress the soul. They push the spirit down into the physical body (we are speaking somewhat symbolically) where it does not wish to be. There is a sense of being crushed down by this low-ceiling environment in which the human being now lives, and it has an unfortunate negative effect on man. And yet, it is appropriate, for this has been a time of a loss from view of the higher reality. The spirit has, in a sense, been beaten down into the physical body of man simply by his own predilections, his own fixing of the attentions on the lower, materialistic and selfish pursuits. Therefore it could not be otherwise. Thus, we are suggesting that with a knowledge of this fact of space, the idea of having more space available to you, you might be able yourself, through meditation and reflecting on what we have said, to come up with improvements on the shape which men now find acceptable. It is a great jump, for example, to go from a straight-sided figure to a pure dome, and many human beings are simply not in a position spiritually or mentally to be able to make that leap. Thus by increments is the way to move men, and this is what we suggest to your contemplation and meditation.

Can you discuss palmistry in terms of showing the nature of the subconscious mind?

The human hand has many wonderful capacities. One of the most marvellous is the fact that it represents, in many detailed ways, the course of the life-pattern being lived. The life pattern is to some extent influenced by choices made on the part of the individual. However, it can be seen from this level that a given direction will be likely to be followed. Thus, although free will is a fact, the working of free will on the earth plane in incarnation is to some extent limited.

In answer to your question, we will discuss the portion of the hand which is referred to as "the percussion". In palmistry terminology, this is the part known as the Mount of the Moon. The Mount of the Moon extends downwardly from the heartline to the bottom of the side of the hand that is underneath the little finger. It does not include the part above the heart line, i.e. between the heart line and the little finger. There is a direct comparison between the Mount of the Moon and the sea's depth from the upper levels to the lower. Think first of the sea. At the highest levels the sun dances upon the water and warms the liquid which is in the upper few feet of this great body of water. The nature of the animals that live in this bright, happy environment is different from those that live further down. As you progress downwardly from the upper surface of the sea, the water cools, the light fades, and the animals which live there change in their appearance. The larger sea animals live lower down. When you reach the very lowest depths there is much that man does not know about the creatures there. Indeed, there are life-forms which would appall man if he were to confront them. This has been prevented up until now because it has not been appropriate for these creatures to make themselves known to the human race.

In the analogy with the "percussion" or Mount of the Moon, the representation is that of the sub-conscious mind. Interestingly, in general symbology, the sea, in addition to representing other factors like the emotional side of the race, is also the symbol for the subconscious of man. The subconscious has many levels just as the sea has. In the highest levels the subconscious contains the detailed practical, everyday, supportive information that is required to keep the conscious mind running smoothly. The talents of driving a car, walking without falling over and so forth — these are functions of the upper portion of the unconscious. You know that when you engage in these activities, your conscious mind does not need to be occupied with them. The reason is simply that the job is turned over to what might be called "the automatic pilot" which is located in the upper portions of the subconscious. Also, in these higher levels are the so-called pigeon-holes for information which is readily retrievable by the conscious mind when you try to think of something which you may have forgotten. Depending upon how far down into the unconscious pigeon-hole arrangement the information has been stored, you will find it more or less easy to retrieve. As you move further down the hand on the Mount of the Moon, you encounter ever deeper, ever darker and ever stranger portions of the unconscious. In certain mental aberrations which are known on the earth, the strange behaviour is related to the fact that there has been a criss-crossing of the energy paths between the conscious and the unconscious, in such a way that the tap-roots for the conscious mind go down to what we might call the "wrong" part of the unconscious. When the information comes up to the conscious mind it is hard to assimilate, it is strange, it produces aberrant behaviour. In the very deepest recess of the unconscious, correlating with the lowest depths of the sea, there live entities which are called Archetypes, which many human beings are not capable of facing. These Archetypes come to the attention through being reflected in the world around one, but are rarely faced squarely by looking within. It is when the conscious mind is not able to accomodate these Archetypes and yet is forced to face them in their total reality that extremely depressive, melancholic, even suicidal tendencies may manifest. We now wish to compare the Mount of the Moon with the headline, which runs from between the thumb and forefinger (at its thickest portion) generally across the hand and toward the Mount of the Moon. The head-line lies normally below the heart-line, i.e. closer to the heel of the hand. The head-line represents a facet of the conscious mind. It is the rational, reasoning, thinking, planning part of the mind. The ending of the head-line, which is normally its thinnest part, represents the tap-root into the unconscious. If a number of hands were examined you would find that some have the head-line tapping into a very high level of the unconscious (by this we mean close to the heart-line, in the direction of the little finger) while others have a head-line which curves downwardly toward the heel and taps into the unconscious at a much deeper level. We do not say that one of these is better than the other, simply that the nature of the tap-root, and its location in terms of position in the unconscious, will have an effect on the mind and on the way in which the conscious intellect functions. Where the head-line taps deeply into the lowest unconscious levels, there is a danger that the Archetypal energies which pass upwardly along the head-line will have the effect of disrupting the conscious mind and causing it to dwell on thoughts akin to those that abide in the lower levels. These thoughts will vary depending upon the individual, but in many cases these energy formations in the lowest level of the unconscious will be of a negative and difficult kind due to the past life experiences. In cases of this kind, where there is a deep tap into the lower levels, you may assume that a struggle in the conscious mind is likely to have to be made in order to come to terms with these darker energies which were formed by that same individual in prior lives. Thus you may look on it as karmic in significance. There are many intermediate levels and these pertain to the kinds of intuitive inspiration which can be derived from one's own past experiences, as these are in many cases stored in the unconscious. Thus, a head-line which ends at about the middle region of the subconscious, as represented by the Mount of the Moon, can be taken as showing a considerable potential for creativity, if only the individual could learn to assimilate the energies which come up along the head-line from the unconscious. In summary, we would state that the Mount of the Moon in palmistry represents the unconscious, and we would emphasize the value of being able to assess the nature of the head-line contact with the unconscious in terms of analyzing the nature of the energy interchange in the conscious mind of the person whose hand is being studied. By using this information you will be in a position to help your brothers to understand why, in many cases, they are called upon to go through a struggle that they will immediately recognize when you speak of it.

Editor's note: In the book, *Symbols,* Hilarion suggests a meditation that takes one through the levels of the mind in order to deal with some of one's Archetypes.

Please comment generally on science in this Century.

The subject of Science is one that is very dear to our hearts as many readers will know. Indeed, the ray along which we transmit this information is precisely that which is instrumental in bringing about the scientific advancements which already have been made and which are going to be made in the years to come.

The greatest error which 20th century scientists have fallen into is their belief that the world about them is made up of tiny separated packets of matter, not connected to each other by any intervening material, and not having anything to do with each other. They believe that the Universe is made up of tiny billiard balls which they call protons, neutrons and so forth which simply bounce against each other and create the various phenomena which they observe in their laboratories. Alas, this error is reflected in man's own mental state at present. Humanity shuts itself off from itself; men carve up the surface of the planet into separate chunks which they say they "own"; they put emotional distance between themselves and others. The direction of Science could not have been any other than what it was, given the materialistic, separative and rivalrous nature of man's philosophy over the past period of time. But with the coming of the New Age, there will be a dawning of a different understanding about the nature of man and of the nature of the universe in which he finds himself. The two will again be parallel, for mankind will understand that it is one family interconnected by the sea of spirit in which all are immersed, and at the same time he will realize that the matter which he sees about him is composed of one substance, *only one substance*, which he will probably call the aether again, as it was called in the last century. For all of matter which he sees around him is simply the condensation of this aether into particular packets which he recognizes as the protons and so forth. But between all of these is the sea of aether, that tenuous, fine, beautiful substance which extends through all of space and which is responsible for every manifestation and every phenomenon which he perceives in the real world. We believe that this recognition of the oneness of all created matter will soon be manifested upon the earth. Indeed we have attempted to paint the picture in its simplest terms in our own books. We are hopeful that these writings will gradually influence the direction of thought among the scientists of the human family and that as the scientists themselves become persuaded of the truth of the matter, so all mankind will come to understand that every being that has been created partakes of a single, central, creative power

46

which he may call God or the Father, in such a way that they are all linked through Him to each other.

Would you please discuss U.F.O's.

The apparitions which many people have seen or claim to have seen in the skies of the earth in the past forty years or so are often mistaken; that is, some of them are due to atmospheric aberrations, to meteors and the like. However, there is a definite percentage of these sightings in which the observer did in fact perceive a vehicle operated by visitors from other parts of this galaxy. It is an extremely complex matter to try to explain fully how these vehicles come to be seen by human beings, or to give a breakdown of the categories of vehicles. There are many kinds, some are of physical matter, others are of astral matter, others are of aetheric matter. There are even some which are of material which does not fall into any of those categories. Likewise, the inhabitants come from vastly differing civilizations. Some are similar to that on the earth; others are strictly mentally oriented; others again are primarily concerned with creation and the act of will which results in something being created. As a general comment, we should point out that some of these vehicles are in the vicinity of earth because of the risk of damage to the fabric of space, due to mankind's dabbling with energies he does not understand. We refer to nuclear explosive energy. These entities who have come to protect man from himself have the ability of literally stopping a nuclear explosion which has begun, or of interfering with the explosive mechanism of a nuclear warhead, in order to prevent an explosion if they wish to do so. Alternatively, they have other means by which to strengthen the fabric of space in the region of a nuclear blast so that there need be no risk of destroying the fabric of the Universe. Finally, we should point out that the observers who have come to this region of space all understand that the human family has placed itself in a dreadful predicament, and that the years to come will shortly be filled with dread and catastrophy for the race. They are prepared to help when they are asked to do so by the Hierarchy above them. And they are now preparing their instruments of healing and rescue for the time when the most serious need arises.

Please elaborate more on the inhabitants of the Center Core of the Earth.

We would rather say only a little about the core and the core experience for humanity, for reasons which we are not allowed at this time to give.

There is indeed a hollow core in the centre of the earth. It is inhabited by many thousands of people. It does contain animals, many of which are in species that are extinct on the earth. It does contain species that never were on the surface of the earth. It is true that many human beings will be taken to the core of the earth during the time of rescue from the chaos that is descending on the earth. However, what we have written in *The Nature of Reality* on this subject is necessarily simplified and condensed and we were not able at that time to sketch the full dimensions of the rescue operation which is to be launched by those who have come from other parts of this galaxy to observe the death throes of human civilization as it now exists on the earth. As to the specific nature of the natural inhabitants of the centre core of the earth, this may be thought of as follows: these souls are human souls but the physical bodies which they inhabit are somewhat different genetically from those of man on the surface. They are taller because of a gravitational difference. The configurations of certain parts of the body will be found to be different by those who spend an appreciable time in the centre core. However, in terms of their civilization, they are at approximately the same level of technical development. They have evolved superior social forms not having anything to do with the forms which man on the surface has devised. We would suggest simple patience and a readiness to accept strangeness in those who are to be taken to the centre core. It will be an experience which is appropriate primarily for those whose minds have been stretched and broadened by the nature of their interests on the surface. You will understand that there are many souls on the surface of the earth who are very good souls in terms of their basic moral outlook on life and their desire to help others, but who are also in many cases very narrow and restricted as to the horizon of possibilities which they can contemplate. We are thinking of the small towns of the United States and Canada; for example, the good farmer who is kind to all but has not really thought much about the magnificent possibilities which could open before the race. Such individuals would find a terrific shock if they were to be presented with the strangeness of life in the core, or of life on the huge mother ships which circle the earth at the present time. And therefore another arrangement has been made. However, this is not an appropriate subject to be discussed through this channel at the present time.

Could you comment on the recent escape of American diplomats from Iran, through the help of the Canadian embassy there?

Yes, the operation of rescue was deliberately encouraged by those on this side who are directly involved in the course of events on the earth. The purpose of this demonstration of practical help by Canadians for Americans was two-fold. The first purpose was to show the world that bravery and courage are not dead; that even in these times of mass fear and the feeling that one can do little to stand in the way of the giant forces which are holding sway in the earth, there is yet opportunity for individuals to stand up and say "enough". This quality will be sorely needed in the trials that lie just ahead. The second purpose for this exercise was to show the Americans particularly that they had at least one staunch friend on which they could rely. It is probable that, during the next five years, an attempt will be made to put pressure on Canada in order to "bully" her into taking certain actions. This pressure will come from Asia. In this time of trial, it will be Canada that will need a friend, and she will find one in the loyal Americans, who will be more than anxious to return the favor that has recently been done by Canada.

Are there any succinct key words or phrases to describe the physical appearance of each Zodiacal sign ascendant?

The subject of Astrology has been much studied by very intelligent human beings over the past milennia and certain areas of it have been codified to an extreme degree, and to a degree which is quite accurate. There are available, on the earth now, certain texts which give a general delineation of the facial and physical characteristics which are to be expected with each rising sign. Many of these can be taken to be accurate. The problem, however, is that the rising sign which many people believe they have is not actually the one which has influenced their physiognomy. The matter is extremely complex. The sign which has influence on the facial features is essentially that which was rising when the soul entered the body in a permanent way. This is not always at the first breath, although in a majority of cases it is very close to the first breath. On the other hand, the first breath sign, if it is different from the soul-entering sign, does also have its influence but not on the physiognomy. The first breath rising point has an influence essentially on the self-image which the personality will develop. Thus you can see that there is a complexity here which makes it difficult to answer the question directly.

JMOJER, PHAETON and the Asteroid belt

50

(The following is based on material provided by *Maurice B. Cooke* and obtained from *Hilarion*. It expands upon the description of the planet *JMOJER* which is contained in *THE NATURE OF REALITY* in the chapter on "Anger".

Until a time 25,000 years ago, there was another planet in the solar system following a roughly circular orbit between Mars and Jupiter. Its average distance from the sun was 200 million miles. It was of physical matter and humanoid beings lived and procreated on its surface. They were ensouled by *fallen* angels, and the purpose of permitting this experiment was to give them an opportunity to improve through physical incarnations in the same way as human souls do on the earth. The planet had the name JMOJER (soft "J" as in French).

The JMOJER race was highly intelligent, and was permitted to develop in many advanced technical areas, including the use of the inert gases to propel space vehicles. Many times they came to the earth, usually for conquest, plunder or colonization. They often were involved in war on the earth.

From time to time highly evolved souls would incarnate on JMOJER to show the way of love and the spiritual goals. The man who was Jesus lived there more than once, and was sacrificed there several times.

Finally, because the experiment on JMOJER was not really succeeding in general, it was decided to destroy the planet. This was accomplished through another planet-like body, PHAETON, which was then in existence and followed a very eccentric orbit of which the perihelion was inside the orbit of the earth, and the aphelion was outside that of Uranus. The orbit of PHAETON was "adjusted" to collide with JMOJER about 25,000 years ago. Both bodies disintegrated on impact and gave rise to the asteroid belt between Mars and Jupiter. Before the collision, a number of JMOJERIANS escaped and came to the earth. However, they succumbed to the earth environment within a few years because the radiation was too strong. The period of crustal movement, mountain building, and submergence of Lemuria on the earth around 25,000 years ago was triggered by a close passage of PHAETON just before it collided with JMOJER.

Would you please explain both the cause and the hidden symbology of the common cold?

It is amusing to us that it should be called the "common" cold for it is all too common among mankind. If men but understood what they were doing which draws this affliction to them, they would rapidly cease to do so, and the "common" cold would become uncommon.

All illness is self-created. Those who suffer, suffer but from themselves. The common cold, as you call it, is an affliction which stems from a very widely distributed thought-form which has suffused itself throughout all regions of the earth's surface where man is living. This thought-form is created by anger which actually results in physical pain upon another — that is, fisticuffs or fighting. When the pain or the focus of the anger is felt by the victim, then the thought-form is created. The thought-form consists partly of anger and partly of the pain. Those who have in past lives or this life deliberately struck others in *anger* (that is the key word) automatically feed the substance of the thought-form. Because the thought-forms are always drawn and attracted to their originators, it is quite natural for this gigantic thought-form related to the cold to be attracted into the bodies of those who feed its substance. When this happens, the symptoms of a cold are felt.

Thus, the way to avoid a cold is primarily to supress and eliminate all feelings of anger and irritation towards another and particularly to avoid striking any other human being in a fit of anger, including children. (It is not a sin to discipline children; indeed, the Creator of the physical body provided a particular portion (we are referring to the

52

buttocks) which is the only part that should be struck if this is ever required. But, when a parent strikes a child in *anger* then a great deal of damage is done at the subconscious level, to the child, and also to the parent).

In summary, we would say that the disposition in many people to catch the common cold is primarily due to the *anger and irritation* feelings which they harbor within them. However, the body itself becomes more inclined to develop cold symptoms when it is subjected to the excesses and abuses of diet which are common in most countries of the world; we refer to meat-eating and the intake of large quantities of concentrated sugars. If these abuses of diet were eliminated, man would find that his tendency to develop cold symptoms would be much lessened.

How does one return the body back to health if one has a cold?

The best advice we can give to the cold sufferer, or the sufferer of any acute illness, is to take no food whatever during the course of the sickness. Cause the body to fast, because the fasting phase of the body's experience will allow it to throw off the invading thought-form more rapidly than would otherwise be the case.

Do dreams have a meaning? Can they be 'directed'?

The question of dreams and their significance is a vast one. We cannot give much more than a simplified overview of the dreaming process and its function in the space allotted here. Many books have already been written on this subject, and we would direct the interested reader to look into the writings of *Jung* in particular, and the work of *Edgar Cayce* on Dreams, for a good treatment of the subject.

The dreaming state is one in which the focus of the individual's higher mind has shifted from the real world to what might be called the "inner world". Many feel, upon hearing these terms, that the inner state is somehow illusory and thus less "valid" than the real world , but this is not the case. Indeed, the *real* world is actually no less an illusion than the dreaming world, since it is merely the condensation of thought (aether), as we have explained in *The Nature of Reality.*

The usual source of the dream material is the subconscious. When an individual dreams, he is usually on the receiving end of a "commentary" by his own subconscious, having to do with certain patterns, problems or characteristics of the individual that are currently manifesting. The dream imagery is always symbolic, or nearly always, and should never be interpreted as directly stating something in the same terms as it is found in the waking state. Secondly, only occasional dreams are prophetic or predictive. The subconscious certainly is aware of the probabilities ahead for the individual, but it will not normally signal to the conscious mind what it sees unless such a signalling is used to try to persuade the conscious mind to *change its course*! Thus, if you have a premonitory dream that does actually come true, the great likelihood is that you *failed* to make a change which the subconscious was hoping you would make. The major exception to this rule relates to dreams which point out the likelihood of death for someone close to you. These dreams are given for the purpose of allowing the conscious mind to come to terms with the idea of the death, and to assimilate it. This will make the actual experience of the death less traumatic.

In a minority of cases, dreams are manipulated by the guides for the purpose of teaching something to the subconscious, or to "act out" a pattern that is contemplated for waking life. In the latter case, there may be doubt as to how the person is likely to react. For example, if it is contemplated to bring you into touch with someone with whom you once had an extremely violent fight, resulting in your death, and if there is some possibility that a meeting again in this life will also lead to violent behavior on your part, then the two of you may be brought together in the dreaming state in order to test your reactions (and possibly that of the other person as well) before arranging the meeting in the physical plane.

The best approach to all dreams initially is to assume that they bear a message for you in symbolic terms, and to use your knowledge of symbols and correlations to work out what that message might be.

As to the matter of manipulating dreams, the best way is to deliberately ask your subconscious for a certain kind of dream which will help you with a problem, etc. You would address your subconscious at night when you go to bed, and repeat what you wish to have at least three times — merely in order to ensure that the subconscious gets the message. For example, if you wish to know details of a prior life in which you knew such-and-such another person, you would ask for this information in the form of a dream, which is to be given just prior to waking so that it will be clearly remembered. The subconscious will then arrange such a dream. However, since the subconscious rarely uses actual events, it may provide you with a *symbolic* representation of the main features of the prior relationship, which it is up to you to interpret.

Can you simplify the nature of matter as discussed in The Nature of Reality?

The nature of matter is not difficult to grasp, if explained with the help of an analogy. The analogy relates to the condensation of water droplets from water vapor in the air. It is a common experience that, when a cold bottle is taken from the refrigerator and left in a warm room, very soon water droplets begin to form around the outside of the glass. The reason for this condensation of water relates to the fact that the air can hold only so much water vapor, depending upon its temperature. The colder the air is, the less water vapor it can hold. Now, in the space very close to the glass of the cold bottle, the air is cooled by the nearness of the bottle, and the cooler layer of air very close to the bottle sides cannot hold as much water vapor as the warmer air further away. For this reason, the water in the cooled air condenses into water droplets, and these then appear on the sides of the bottle. Since one cannot see the vapor in the air, it is as if the water "materialized" from nothing.

The water vapor contained in the atmosphere can be compared to what we shall call the "aether" of space itself. Extending throughout all of three-dimensional space, even between the stars and within the structure of the atom, is this tenuous, fine, stretchable material. It cannot be seen, any more than water vapor can be seen. But just like water vapor, it has two 'states' of being: it can exist in the expanded and more rarefied state in which it is invisible; or it can condense just like water droplets condense, to form a much more compact and dense 'droplet' of aether. This droplet of aether is what scientists call the proton — the basic building block of all matter.

Thus, all material everywhere in this three-dimensional universe is composed of tiny droplets of condensed aether, which are located in a "sea" of more expanded aether. It can therefore be seen that the *only thing that exists* in terms of the material universe is the aether, and that matter is merely a particular state of this substance.

Can you discuss lightning and its meaning?

There are many realms beyond man's comprehension at the present. There are the realms of the nature spirits, the realms of the Devas, the realms of the creatures which he has occasionally seen and which he has called Leprechauns and fairies, and so forth. There are also Kingdoms which are of material substance, namely the mineral, vegetable and animal kingdoms, with man being a fourth kingdom above those three. The elements of nature are controlled by the nature spirits. We do not confuse these with the Devas which represent a different kingdom or group.

The nature spirits are neither good nor evil. They are neutral. They obey the directives given to them by entities in the Hierarchy above man who wish to use the nature spirits' power in order to bring karmic patterns to bear upon mankind. The principal effects which are employed this way are those of the tornado, those of the hurricane, those of lightning, those of the flood, and those of the great storms and tempests which rage from time to time on the earth. All of these focuses of power are controlled by specific nature spirits. In times past many of the initiates or adepts among mankind understood how to command these nature spirits and could force them to act or not to act at will. But man has lost the knowledge which he once had and now there is no one who can command the spirits of the storm, the lightning and so forth. The command comes from the level of the guides and guardians of the race. They have the mental power and the knowledge by which to require these spirits to carry out certain specific functions for karmic purposes. When a tornado touches down on one house and destroys it but leaves the adjacent house unharmed, you can be certain that the sparing of the other house was part of a definite plan with karmic associations. The same is true of the lightning when it is used to strike specific buildings or to cause harm to human beings. Lightning is never allowed to randomly cause damage to man; it is only allowed to cause damage when this is a karmic necessity.

Can you comment on the validity of the aspect known as the quintile (72 degrees of arc) and whether it does in fact indicate special talents?

We are aware that some astrological researchers believe that there is such an aspect as the quintile and indeed the guides and guardians will occasionally make use of this aspect when it is particularly close and when they think there is some likelihood that the incarnated personality will later wish to review his chart with an astrologer familiar with the quintile aspect. However, we stress that the primary aspects of square, oppostition, trine, sextile, semi-sextile and inconjunct are by far the more powerful in terms of the likelihood that their meanings apply to the chart. You will often find that if the quintile of 72 degrees is also considered along with the other primary aspects, a great criss-crossing of lines and influences will take place, to such an extent as to obscure the more important of the aspects. We therefore suggest that the astrologer adhere to the basics, for the guides and guardians have done the same in selecting the chart.

Can you give more elaboration on the meanings of the marks on the ends of the fingers than was given in SEASONS OF THE SPIRIT?

The meanings of the marks on the finger ends have been quite well explained in our book, at least in a general way. There are additional connections that could be elaborated on, but we think it would be best at this time to limit such further explanation to one area only. It is too early to give the next plateau in this subject, as too few have understood fully the significance of what we have already made available.

The additional area we would like to give here has to do with the little finger especially. We have not explained fully in our book that *each* phalange of *each* finger has to do with a particular lesson. The little finger of man has reference to the lessons of sex, acceptance of menial work, and judging others. The end or nail phalange pertains to the sexual lessons generally. This we have already explained.

The middle phalange has to do with the idea of being able to accept a position or job which the individual feels somehow beneath him, or not up to his capacities, i.e. not what he deserves (as far as he is concerned). However, many people have an exaggerated idea of what they deserve in this area, one that is not a true reflection of their actual abilities or talents. The *only* way for most people to come to a correct assessment of their own capabilities is for them to be forced to undergo a period during which they are held back, as it were, and forced to "apprentice" for longer than they would like. Only in such a situation will most individuals be prompted to assess themselves honestly, in order to find out whether they really do merit anything better than the job they have. If the middle phalange is quite short, compared to the other two, this denotes a frustration and impatience with being held back in the job or career. If the phalange is heavily marked with cross-lines traversing across the finger, these denote times in the life when career or job difficulties will be experienced in order to cause a more realistic assessment of the self's capabilities in terms of work. We have explained the timing proportions in our book, *Seasons of the Spirit.*

The innermost phalange relates to the tendency to be judgemental of others. This trait is never desirable, of course. The Scriptural admonition is "JUDGE NOT!", and any who indulge in this form of negative thinking — whether the judgemental thought is expressed or not — are simply enwrapping themselves in a cocoon of dark and prejudicial thoughts which act to keep out the light of spiritual truth, and hide the individual from the higher concepts of life's purpose. As we have explained in our books, THOUGHTS ARE THINGS, and negative judgements of others are among the *most damaging 'things' of this kind* that could possibly be imagined, because of the retardation of spiritual progress which they cause. Until the cloak of negative thinking can be swept away, there is little chance for the individual to even encounter the truths of the spirit, let alone understand or accept them.

Can you comment on card reading, in reference to regular playing cards, and the Tarot?

The question of card-reading is a complex one, as we have said in *The Nature of Reality*. The cards speak to the reader by means other than the simple "reflex action" of the universe, as is the case with the I-Ching, for example. Indeed, the entities who originally gave the gift of the cards to the human family are required by their own promise to continue to make the cards "work" in the predictive sense for the remainder of the period during which man's own psychic and "seeing" faculty remains dormant. After this faculty has been awakened in all men, as it will have been within the next 100 years, there will be no further need for the cards and the method by which they may be used for a glimpse of the future probabilities.

This introduces a critically important point, namely that the cards always show the most likely events *as seen at the time when the question was asked*. These probabilities may change as time goes on in response to free-will decisions, and such changes can falsify the predictive nature of card reading to some extent. And yet such falsification is far from an undesirable turn of events in many cases. There is a deep understanding among occultists that "The best prophet is a false prophet". This curious saying contains a kernal of great truth. For what would be the purpose of having prophecy when the prophesied events always came true? Are men any better off knowing about disaster or fortune one day or one week ahead of the actual event? No, the purpose of prophetic warnings — and this includes the very warnings that are found in our own books — is to prompt men to change to such a degree that the forseen events are much lessened in severity, and perhaps need not arrive at all. In other words, it is the great hope of the high entities who arranged for some men to have the gift of prophecy, that their brothers could be induced to change evil and negative ways through hearing about what awaited them if the evil continued. Any other purpose for prophecy simply does not make sense.

To return to the cards, we may say that although the Tarot is the "best" deck in general use for prophetic purposes, nonetheless any deck of cards (even hand-lettered pieces of cardboard which the reader may wish to make for himself) *will* be manipulated by the high entities who have bound themselves to this service, to the greatest extent possible, consistent with the nature of what the cards show and the understanding of the person attempting to read them. In fact, a small experiment will convince any doubters that what we say here is true: Simply obtain ten equal-sized blank pieces of cardboard material — about the shape of playing cards — and mark them with the numbers zero to nine (one side only). Then proceed to use them as a predictive guide. Ask the cards any question you wish, then shuffle and cut them. The number you turn up will always have some meaning in terms of an answer, although if your question is obscure or in some area where the number significances do not shed much light, you may have to hunt awhile for the correct interpretation. The reader may wish to use, as his basic approach to the meaning of the numbers, the scheme set out in our book, *Symbols.* This should give him the broadest and most useful numerical system for interpretation. A final point to be made is that the cards will rarely, if ever, repeat themselves when the question is repeated. The entities who manipulate the cards for the reader are not required to repeat a given manipulation, but they may, if they wish, add some further glimpse into the answer to the question that has been asked. Indeed, only rarely do they become so exasperated with the doubtful attitude of a reader as to actually stop manipulating the cards altogether.

We are not, of course, suggesting that a number system is superior to the Tarot, or even to the normal playing cards. The Tarot was designed by men strongly overshadowed by the influence of the great entities who conceived the idea of the cards in the first place and the present-day result of their labors is without doubt the most useful and broad-ranging tool for prediction that there could possibly be.

Can you briefly comment on what the Hilarion Series is all about?

(by the Publisher of Marcus Books)

The Hilarion series consists of four books (now 16 — 1985), which have been dictated telepathically through Toronto businessman *Maurice B. Cooke* by the entity known as *Hilarion. Hilarion* is a name known in Theosophical writings, and is said to be the entity in charge of detailed scientific and occult knowledge for man on this planet.

The purpose of the information in these books is to address the conscious, reasoning intellect and to offer a logical, coherent explanation of 1) the purpose of man's life on the earth, and 2) the nature of the reality in which he finds himself.

Because of the narrow and skeptical attitude of many people, these books have the additional task of expanding the horizon of possibilities which the human mind can encompass. For this reason many pages of each book are dedicated to stretching the imagination of the reader. Since science is particularly under the influence of this source, it is not surprising that certain parts of these books provide some new insights into the physical sciences, and even describe the manufacture of apparatus operating on wholly new principles totally outside the framework of conventional physics.

Lastly, the books in this series of transmissions stress repeatedly the great risk of immanent global catastrophe: Unless there occurs a spontaneous reawakening of spiritual purpose among mankind, unless a broad movement away from the unworthy pursuits of selfishness and materialism arises, then a time must come when all of man's systems — military, political and economic — will disintegrate before the onslaught of war and natural upheaval. No longer, say the books, is there any significant likelihood that the great purging of the earth can be avoided. The negative energies which humanity has built up over many ages must break loose and wreak the havoc that is their very nature.

Can you give a commentary on the purpose of life?

There are many purposes behind every manifestation within the real world. Every tree, every flower, every animal, has its path to follow and its lessons to learn. This applies even to the rocks, the mountains, the streams, the oceans. For each of these too is a living entity in the spiritual sense. But in terms of man, there is a special purpose which is different from the purposes of these other life forms. In the case of mankind as a group, the purpose is to manifest a balanced triangle of mental, emotional and physical attributes to the maximum level of which it is capable. The manifestation of the great Triangle of Being at the level of man is an undertaking of the greatest importance, not only to humanity but to other galactic races, to the guides and guardians who have helped humanity through the long pilgrimage from innocence through darkness to the present, and finally to the higher realms as well. It is from these higher realms that the destinies of the races of men are directed. It was known early in the cycle of the present Great Year that few of the races of men in the various star-systems had volunteered to develop the emotional or "love" side of the triangle. This was because of a fear that they would become entrapped in *negative* emotion. They therefore chose to develop the mental attributes instead. But mankind on this planet has offered itself as the main experiment in the development of the heart side of the triangle at the "level of man". Because the task has been difficult, an additional help has been forthcoming for humanity. This help has come through many great entities who have descended to the earth to live and to show the way, and often to die at the hands of mankind. But soon the experiment will show its fruits. It is beyond any doubt now that the human race on the planet earth will demonstrate, to all other races of man from other parts of this galaxy, the beauty, the glory, the power and the majesty of the love of God, for humanity alone will have learned how to flood love upon all creatures. They will have learned this in the only way possible, for they will have *taught it to themselves*. That is the purpose of life on this planet in terms of humanity as a group.

But each individual soul who is incarnated among the race of men has its own set of purposes as well. From the individual standpoint, the overall purpose is to rise to higher levels of development, of evolution, of spirituality and of understanding. These levels in a sense are piled upon each other, rising up out of sight like the rungs of a ladder that disappears upwardly. When one set of lessons is learned the soul moves to a higher circuit of learning and begins on the next set of lessons. This process is the same for all beings in all of the great cycles of manifestation within the real world. Only the details of the specific lessons at specific times may change or be different from one group to the next, yet all are engaged in increasing their awareness, or vibrations, or spirituality . . . whatever you may wish to call it. And all will ultimately succeed, for that is the master plan for all manifestations. Looked on from a final point of view, the goal and purpose of life is to return to the source which originally projected each individual soul. This source is so high and so great that earth language cannot begin to describe its majesty. It is to this that all are destined one day to return. But only after what may appear to be almost endless cycles of learning.

Would you elaborate for us what is involved in being used as a spiritual channel — as Maurice Cooke is, for example?

The nature of any source that is contacted in this way is something that can only be understood by way of comparisons. In the practice of meditation, for example, there is much information that is passed through one's own guide, but in many cases the ideas are also embedded in one's own subconscious, from where they can enter the conscious mind. In the case of the present channel, there is a strong factor of contribution from the subconscious of the one through whom this is coming (*Maurice Cooke*); however his subconscious has been "trained" so-to-speak, through many teaching situations taking place primarily during sleep. Thus, we have been able to plant into the subconscious of this channel much of the material which we know will be asked sooner or later, and from this storehouse it is possible for the channel to draw up the answers that are sought, in many cases. We then do not have as much to do in terms of energy output. We may put it this way: where something must be transmitted which is entirely new to this channel, and not already available to his subconscious, we must expend greater energy in getting the ideas through to the conscious mind. Where the subconscious already is familiar with the area of the question, we merely have to guide the "automatic" answering process which takes place whenever the subconscious is asked for information.

This leads to an interesting point:

Anyone can deal with his own subconscious in exactly the same way, and obtain answers to questions which are already programmed into the subconscious. The guides of the individual will often try — with greater or lesser success — to influence the answering process in the way that we do for this channel, and thus something akin to the procedure now taking place with this channel can be experienced by anyone.

Would you describe how we can best help Mother Earth during the coming time of crisis?

The time of choosing which stands before the race also includes the great entity on whose surface humanity exists. This is something which has not been fully explained through any channel hitherto. We are pointing out that the Earth Being herself has a choice which she will confront at the peak of the darkness soon to descend. That choice is whether she will continue to harbor the human species or not. For literally, it could happen that the Earth will refuse to be any longer the home of a group that is so primitive in terms of soul-evolution that it would devour other sentient beings for its food, scar the body of the Earth terribly with its weapons of mass destruction, and wage all-out war on its own species. If the earth decides to be done with her association with humanity, she will be allowed to have her way, for this beautiful being has suffered much at the hands of man.

None of the other life-experiments which she has harbored has ever treated her with such disdain, or with so little love and consideration. For man does not know consciously that *the Earth is a living being*. If he but understood this great truth, he surely would not have despoiled her of her riches, scarred her lovely covering mantle, or exploded devastating bombs within her very body.

If the race of man wishes to continue to inhabit this most beautiful of all planets in the galaxy, then he must tell her that this is so. One way is to stop forever the depredations and the pain which he causes her. But another — and possibly the most essential — is to communicate directly with this great and shining entity, and tell her that truly man wishes her to remain with him, and that the race will lend her its own strength and commiseration during the trials and pain which soon will come.

The way to achieve this is through the technique of meditation. During the meditative experience, those who have become seekers after the truth of the spirit may consciously address the earth being, and assure her of their love and support.

There is one point more that we should make: When the

darkness of the Tribulation blackens to its worst point, at the very end of the great trial, the earth itself will be alone and without the constant reminder of the Godhead which it has had for all of its existence. We refer to the extinction of the central sun. This time of blackest night for the Earth Being will be the same in its terror as was the "giving up of the Christ Spirit" when the Master was on the cross. At that point, the Earth Being will need man's love and thoughts as she has never needed these before. If the race can together come to the rescue of the mother planet, there will be no doubt that she will decide that her destiny is to remain as the lovely harbor for humanity that she has always been.

Can you comment on the question of TWIN-SOULS, as to whether they often incarnate together, and whether they can be recognized?

Yes. The question of twin flames or twin souls is a very complex one. The notion that each soul has a particular other soul that is its twin is in general true, although there are many others for each soul who could be thought of as being almost as close as the actual twin soul. This arises because of the numerous contacts between the various souls in previous incarnations. The actual twin soul, then, exists, generally speaking. The idea of the twin has inspired many stories in fables and other areas where two souls are described as being "perfect" for each other. We refer to the Romeo and Juliet story, the Tristan and Isolde legend, etc. These idealized tales are based on the longing which each soul has to find again the perfect mate that it once knew. For in fact there was once a time when each soul had a perfectly matched "mate" soul, with which it lived in complete harmony. This occurred after the time of the sexual division to which we refer in our books, but before the time of the Temptation. In this brief time of bliss, all matched souls lived in total harmony not only with their own mates, but with all of the other realms of nature and the higher kingdoms as well.

The rule under which the twin soul manifests on the earth now is the following. It is normally not permitted for both twin souls to be in incarnation at the same time. The reason for this prohibition is simply that, should they meet each other while in incarnation, and become mated in the flesh, the complete harmony which they would be able to develop within a very short time would short-circuit the learning process for which they came to the earth. In other words, the purpose of physical existence is to go through difficulties and *difficult relationships*, in order to be prompted to soften the characteristics that clash with those of the other person. But if the blend between two people is almost complete, no such impetus for improvement is present.

In regard to the question of how to recognize the twin soul, we are permitted to say only that these are usually born with sun signs that are square to each other. For example Cancer and Libra. Very often, there is a considerable age difference, such that there is less temptation to come together than if the ages were close. Also, it sometimes happens that the twin souls are born as parent and child, in order to place another obstacle to their coming together in the sense of lovers. In the latter case, it is intended that such a union *not* take place, and the placing of the two together in such an arrangement is for the purpose of allowing them to manifest other sides to their relationship, and sometimes for help from one to the other.

Can you discuss the Olympic Games — then and now? Please refer to the current problems.

The Olympic Games were intended to allow man to give expression to the rivalrous and aggressive instincts which he shares to some extent with the animals, and this purpose was largely served in the earlier years of the Olympic movement. It was thought, by those who guide these matters from a higher plane, that by allowing an expression such as this, the various nations of the world would not have to resort to warfare in order to allow the aggressive instincts out into the open. However, man's capacity for hatred and contempt for his brothers has far surpassed what was expected in the early years, and the games have become a mere pawn in the struggle for dominance among nations. For this reason, it has been decided that the Olympic movement must be halted for the current phase of chaos and warfare in the earth, so that the pure light of the Olympic ideal will not be tainted and dragged through the mire of bitterness and hatred which will characterize man's dealings with his brothers for the next few years.

Please comment on the current Afghanistan situation.

The situation in that unfortunate country is no more and no less than is appropriate under the great Law of Karma as it applies to the souls who have incarnated there. These souls are, without exception, those who have never learned to give up warring ways, never learned that there is only one way for man to live in peace — in a spirit of love and brotherhood among all of the human family. In life after life, they have resorted to war, conquest and pillage — never thinking of the desperation and tragedy that have followed their wars in the lands that were conquered. But the wheel turns full circle always. Now it is their turn to taste the bitter defeat, so that they will perhaps see at last the fruits that war always brings. Their land will be virtually absorbed by the Russian Bear in the months ahead, and all Afghanistan people who continue to resist and defy the Russian conquerors will be crushed beneath the might of the Russian war machine.

But for her part in this annihilation of an entire people, Russia too will suffer greatly. No act of war or conquest is ever lifted from the Karma of any country, even in cases where that conquest is being used to set aside Karma for the conquered people. Russia will be led to play a tragic part in the dreadful trials that lie just ahead for the race. She will be drawn into the very crucible of the Tribulation. As a result of that intense fire, Russia will again be purified, but very little will remain of her population — only those few who have perceived the truth about the human condition, and who have realized that man must live together in brotherhood — or else he will not live at all.

In your books, you refer to the desirability of trying to achieve a balance between the male and female character-istics in each personality. Do you have any practical suggestion as to how this may be attained?

The question is relatively easy to answer, for the greatest obstacle to the achievement of this inner balance is the belief which most people have that they do not possess any inner traits which correspond to the opposite sex. There is a current tendency to over-stress the sexual roles of man and woman, and this has led to a suppression of the traits which belong to the other sex. As a result, a considerable tension and distortion arises within the personality, which actually makes that individual far more dependent on "having someone to be with" than he would be if he found and encouraged the "other-sex" traits within himself. We are not referring to traits of effeminate behavior for men, or to the mannish attitudes of some women. We are talking of the "animus" and "anima" packages which we have described in our book *Seasons of the Spirit.* The animus is that package of male traits which includes adventurousness, athleticism, practical creativity and intellectual achievement. The Anima represents the nurturing, receptive and emotional side of the human being. It is intended that both men and women develop all of these admirable qualities within themselves, and anyone who cared to try this experiment in self-expansion would quickly see the manifold advantages which would result — in terms of greater happiness, self-confidence and the ability to relate to others.

What are the actual inborn differences between men and women as compared to the culturally conditioned differences?

The inborn differences depend on what is projected into the personality by the soul. Not all men have the same package of male traits, nor are all women equally "feminine". It often happens that a soul, for the purposes of learning or of balancing its own complex of characteristics, will project into a female personality much more of the masculine side of itself than would be "normal", while many men (particularly at the present time in the earth) are carrying around an extra quantum of femaleness within. The purposes for the various mixtures are too varied and too complex to be sketched here. We will say merely that there is such a variance in terms of male traits in men and female ones in women that to delineate a "normal" level of one or the other would inevitably be inadequate to provide a true grasp of the process under discussion.

Should we begin to gather together, secure land and try for self-sufficiency if, as you say, our social systems and institutions are about to collapse? In other words, should we prepare for the upcoming Tribulation?

The best way to prepare for that which lies before the human race is to concentrate all of one's efforts on learning the truths of the spirit, on helping one's brothers, and on coming to an understanding of the purpose of one's life. There is an admonition in the scriptures by which one is advised to seek first the Kingdom of Heaven and it is promised that all else will be added. This is literally true in the most real sense possible. In terms of one's own safety, one's own well-being, it is the case that no individual need be concerned about those areas, so long as he fixes his attention on the truths of the spirit, on the necessity for raising the vibrational level, the understanding and the spirituality of oneself and of the race as a whole. Any who decide in their hearts that this is the path they wish to tread and who ask in meditation or in direct prayer for a way to be shown how they can be of service to others in this greatest time of need for the human race, will find that their prayers will be answered immediately. Opportunities to perform this service will literally flood into thier lives. If they merely take these opportunities as they come, these individuals may be certain that no harm and no need will ever visit them.

There are, however, practical considerations over the next few years and we would be happy to set out a few guidelines. In the first place it is likely that sources of concentrated protein will become quite scarce within a few years. When this happens, those who have insulated themselves from the need for concentrated protein will not suffer the difficulties associated with sudden withdrawal from these sources. But many who continue to eat large quantities of meat, for example, through the next few years, will be put to a severe test when it becomes necessary to give up these sources of meat. There are other ways to protect oneself as well: for example, taking care that one's resources are relatively liquid in form, but here again we are touching on areas which are not necessary to the service of others. If that can be accomplished then all of these other facets will be taken care of. *There is a law of a very high nature to that effect and that law never fails.*

Can you comment on the recent influx of Cuban refugees into the United States, and its esoteric significance?

We will explain the Cuban experience in terms of a general process which has been going on for some decades, and will continue for another few years. This is the process of separation. Those who are even potentially able to rise to a higher level of insight and spirituality regarding the human condition are separating from those who cannot. It is a fork in the road, a choice of a most fundamental nature which is being put before many peoples in many places. In the case of Cuba the souls born to life on that island are largely those who have not been able to perceive clearly that men should be free and left free by others, that there should not be an interference in the life pattern of an individual, either by other individuals or by an organized group, for example the government, or any particular controlling organization. The Cubans as a whole have been forced to live under a regime which does seek to interfere in and control the lives of the citizens of the island. The control and interference are such that those who have even a glimmer of understanding of the higher truths would be able to see that this constitutes a serious infringement of the natural God-given right of each individual to be free.

It is these few for the most part who are escaping from the island at the present time. This constitutes a separation between those who have a slight potential to understand the real truths about humanity and those who have decided that they do not wish to know. The island of Cuba lies on a very sensitive location in the earth, along with the other islands in the chain. The coming upheavals will cause much damage, and the difficulties that come to the island and to the people who remain on it will be part of the great setting aside of Karmic burden which the race will be accomplishing in the next few years.

Can you give more information on the Equinox/Solstice times of the year, relative to the Hierarchy and Meditation?

There are many key times at which various levels of the Hierarchy of this planetary system align themselves in terms of vibration with those upon the earth plane. This alignment is accomplished primarily to allow energies from these higher levels to flood the earth so that they may be used by human beings in incarnation. For the most part, these pivitol times occur at full moon, for example, Wesak and others. Indeed, every full moon has a special purpose in terms of a particular level of the Hierarchy. Each one is used by a different level for the purpose of allowing energies from that level to be made available to the earth plane. However, at the times of the solstices and equinoxes, there is another process which takes place. This is a process by which the earth entity is allowed to rid itself of poisons and toxins as you might call them, which it has accumulated over the preceding quarter. It is similar to the cleansing of the etheric body by water. At these times of Solstice/ Equinox, the geometry of the earth and the sun reaches a *node*, so to speak, in its circuit. At these nodal locations a special "wash" of energy from the sun sweeps over the earth entity and carries away many of the poisons that have built up in her due to her own emotional nature. The latter is very similar to that of man. This is a further evidence that the earth is a being very much like an individual human being, but on a much larger scale.

Could you elaborate on the esoteric meaning of the upcoming Quebec referendum? (May 1980)

Your country is a shining star of moral uprightness and kindness for the children of the earth. It was planned from the beginning that Canada would show how two peoples could learn to live together in harmony and brotherhood and love. Your country stands now before the gravest choice which it has ever faced, for she must decide whether to remain united and strong, or whether to become divided and weak. We cannot say how this choice will be made, for man has free will. In the case of political events, the free will is of a greater latitude than in other situations. If the decision made by those in Quebec is to seek a more independent role, it is likely that the rest of the country will change to accomodate Quebec, without actually causing the country to break into two parts. If the decision is made in the other way, then ultimately a similar result will come about. We have stated that the country stands before a great choice, but we think that the end result of this process, regardless of how the referendum is decided, will be substantially the same: a change of sorts in the structure of the country, but not a complete division between its parts.

What is the common cause of baldness and can a true cure be found in the near future?

The loss of hair from the human head is a very complex subject. Most of those who suffer this loss are men and in almost all cases it will be found that the father or grandfather of the man also had a tendency to lose hair from the head. However, it is more complex than that. The hair of the human head constitutes hundreds of thousands of energy pathways at the etheric level. It is the etheric energy flowing outwardly from the head which ultimately causes the hair to be flat and lifeless in some, or full of life and bounce in others. It is strictly a question of what is happening at the etheric level within the head that determines the nature of the hair. It also determines whether the hair will fall out, at least to some degree. We have said that the tendency is genetically inherited most of the time and this is true; but the reason for the genetic flaw developing in the lineage of the man who is now bald relates to a repeating pattern of short-circuiting etheric head energy, which was a pattern adopted by his forefathers. The short-circuiting of the etheric energies of the head is largely due to the focusing of attention on the world and materialism after reaching an age when the mind should have begun to seek higher into more rarefied levels, into philosophy and so forth. Thus, in one sense, a man is a victim of his genetic inheritance in the sense that the "sins" so to speak, of the fathers are transmitted down the generations as indicated in the scriptures. But in another sense, the person who is now bald can to some extent help alleviate his problem, by raising the attention of his mind to more lofty pursuits than those of the world and the world's aims. One of the main focuses of attention which draws the man's mind downwardly is that of *sexual pre-occupation*. It is for this reason that many observers have remarked that men who have a strong sexual drive tend to be those who lose hair from the head. It is not exactly the sexual drive itself which causes the loss of hair, however, the excessive preoccupation with sexuality or materialsm or any of the facets of worldly life causes an atrophying of the etheric pathways along which the hair grows, and when this energy dies away, the same happens to the hair.

Can a comment be given about the need of a great number of people to wear eyeglasses to correct vision?

The need to use additional means to help focus the eyes arises physiologically from a combination of two things: one is the inability of the lens of the eye to accomodate to various distances, the other is the inability of the eyeball to literally change its length as a result of the pull of various muscles. The changing of the length of the eyeball alters the distance between the lens and the retina, and this helps the eye to focus on objects at various distances. In terms of the higher realities, the inability to focus the eyes on objects at certain distances, or indeed any eye malfunction, refers generally to an inability to see some particular facet of reality or of oneself. The difficulty with sight is always intended to remind the individual that there is something which he is not perceiving or is not assimilating properly. Depending on which eye is the more strongly involved, it can be concluded whether it is the female or the male side of experience which is not seen clearly. This is in accordance with the scheme given in *Seasons of the Spirit* by which the right eye refers to the male package of characteristics and the female package is indicated by the left.

Please comment on the disease, Autism.

This condition arises in those souls who have failed, in previous lives, fully to integrate themselves with society. They have, in most cases, chosen to live separate and apart from their fellows, often leading the life of a hermit. It was not meant that any human soul should cut itself adrift from the main body of humanity. The "cure" which has been devised by the guides who tend the human flock is to gather the powerful thought energies of isolation and separation which the hermit soul had projected in its earlier lives, and to cause these energies to incarnate along with the entering soul, as part of the aetheric body itself. As a result, any clairvoyant who examines an autistic person will immediately see the evidence of these negative aetheric energies in the aura. The self-absorbed behavior and the difficulty in relating to others, which are usually part of autism, stem from the influence of the powerful energies of isolation which are bottled up within the envelopes or vehicles of the soul in this life.

Through such an experience, the soul *meets itself*, and sees clearly the nature of its previous tendencies. The best approach for those who must interact with the autistic child or person is to constantly show and *feel* love for that soul. It is love alone which can bridge the gulf which these individuals have set up between themselves and the rest of humanity.

Can the aura be perceived through various mechanical devices available on the market, or only through the third eye?

The ability to perceive auras and other aetheric manifestations is the birthright of every human born to the earth plane. The inability of many to see at this level is due mainly to the subconscious training and the belief which many hold that there is nothing there to be seen. Also, there is the fact that the nature of the imagery picked up clairvoyantly is different from the imagery seen by the physical eyes. Many people do in fact see with the third eye, but they dismiss the images as a malfunction of the retina, dizzyness, or the like. For example, there are few individuals who could not see the dancing spots in the air quite easily, just by gazing for a few minutes at a patch of blue sky. Many millions *have* noticed these phenomena, but have assumed them to be due to "tricks" being played by their eyes.

With regard to the specific question, we can say that there are no devices currently available which can transform the higher wavelengths into vibrations capable of being seen by the physical eyes. There have been attempts to make filters designed to cut out all visible light and to allow through only ultra-violet light, and for a few individuals these filters have prompted the awakening of a rudimentary ability to see into the higher spectra with the *physical* eyes.

But the best way is to open one's own third eye. This can be done by following a simple program and by applying effort. It is likely that a machine will be developed that will be able to display for the physical eyes that which now only the third eye can see, but by the time such a machine is developed it will have become redundant due to the manifestation of clairvoyance spontaneously among millions and millions of human beings within the next few decades.

Please comment on the effects and importance of fasting.

This topic is of course a very broad one. Not only are there many different kinds of fasts that can be undergone, but the effects of a given form of fast can vary from person to person.

Let us begin by stating unequivocally that the benefits of regular fasting are far greater than those of any other preventive technique now known, including diet supplements, mineral and vitamin therapy, and exercise. Indeed, there are certain holy men in the east who have kept their physical bodies in top condition for over two hundred years merely by the judicious use of fasting.

The purpose of fasting is essentially to allow the body to rid itself of accumulated toxins, mucous and extraneous materials which have accumulated over the period since the previous fast. Since most individuals in the western countries have *never* fasted, it follows that they will have accumulated large amounts of such detrimental material in their bodies by the time they reach adulthood.

What many people do not realize is that fasting is a *natural* mode for the body, one which was designed to help promote health and well-being in the physical vehicle. It was assumed, when the current physical "model" was designed, that individuals incarnating into it would fast on a regular basis, thereby keeping their bodies clean. Teachings to this effect were given by the leaders of man's groups, and by direct revelation at a later date. However, outside of certain eastern cultures, the notion that fasting helps promote bodily health and longevity is virtually unknown.

And yet it is a natural mode, as we have said. When the body fasts, it switches over into an operational sequence which allows it to remove from its tissues the stored poisons that have accumulated. Since the digestive apparatus has been totally or partially shut down, such a cleansing operation can take place. Ordinarily, when not fasting, the energy required for digestion is so great that the cleansing operation cannot be undertaken.

The poisons stored in various bodily tissues are drawn out into the lymph system initially, and from there are dumped into the bloodstream. The kidneys operate to remove these poisons from the blood, and are aided by the other eliminative systems of the body: the lungs, the skin and the colon. Because the kidneys are working at a higher level than normal, many individuals find that their backs become sore when they fast. Such individuals would have quite a high level of toxin accumulation, requiring extra work from the renal system. Also for such highly toxic individuals, the overloading of the bloodstream with toxins will often cause severe headaches. It is interesting that when the body develops a *fever*, the same two symptoms are also present: headache and kidney soreness. This is due to the fact that fever is a device used by the body *to force its spiritual inhabitant to fast*. Fever is not, as some medical sources contend, an attempt by the body to "burn out" the source of the illness, whether viral or bacterial. It is universally the case that, when a person is running a fever, he does not wish to eat. In fact, the smell of food is often nauseating. But the body *can* take liquids (usually) and thus what is happening during a fever-fast, is that the body is promoting a particular kind of food-deprivation for itself, one which compares to what is called a juice fast.

Juice Fasting

When one undertakes a juice fast, the procedure is to remove all solid food from the diet for the duration of the fast, and to take only juices. There are two sub-classes under juice-fasting. The first involves taking mainly fruit juices, whether grape, apple, orange or whatever. The effect of a fruit juice fast is to deprive the body of all food materials except for water and sugar. The water is the base material for all fruit juices, and the sugar is present either as glucose (grape) or fructose (most other fruits). By taking sugar in this form, one is supplying carbohydrate for energy, and is not requiring the body to transform adipose (fatty) tissue in order to keep its energy level up. Such fasts are particularly suitable for those who are not overweight, and whose bodies do not have large quantities of stored fats that can be consumed during a fast.

The other form of juice fast is one in which only (or mainly) vegetable-derived juices are taken. Here again the essential water source is provided, but the carbohydrate source is very minimal. Vegetables have significantly less sugar content than fruits. The main reason for undertaking this non-fruit juice fast is to keep the minerals in the body in balance, and to keep a low level of sustenance entering the system. During such a fast, which is more suited to those who are overweight, the body is forced to convert adipose or fatty tissue to burn for energy, and weight loss usually occurs if the fast is continued long enough.

Fruit Fasting

A form of semi-fast which suits many who are not overweight is that in which only whole fruit is eaten. This does not include bananas or other pulpy fruit. Tomatoes can be included. The purpose of such a regime is to allow the body to keep its energy level up and to provide solids for the digestive tract, while still requiring the body to do without protein or fats. There are many people, particularly in the western culture, whose digestive tracts have a tendency to malfunction in the absence of a regular throughput of solid material. Constipation or diarrhea can result, along with abdominal sensitivity or pain. There is really little difference between a fruit fast and a fruit *juice* fast in terms of the requirements placed upon the body, but the presence of solids in the intestines does take away some energy that could otherwise be used in the fasting (cleansing) process.

Water Fasting

This is an extreme form of fasting, in which the body is placed under considerable strain. Being a fast, the body does of course begin to rid itself of toxins. However, the demands placed upon the liver, kidneys and heart by this form of fast make it unsuitable for many people. We do not recommend that anyone undertake a prolonged water fast (i.e. longer than 4 days) without proper medical supervision.

Protein Deprivation

We now wish to discuss what is, for people in the western cultures, the most significant aspect of any of the forms of fast which we have discussed. That is the fact that, in any fast, the body is immediately faced with a cut-off of protein. We have stated in our books that the body does not need protein, and that the liver is capable of recycling virtually *all* of the body's protein without requiring any significant regular supplement of outside protein, and this is true. However for almost everyone in a meat-eating culture, this recycling ability has been lost, and the liver is not in a condition in which this could take place. Most North Americans, for example, have eaten so much protein all their lives, that the recycling ability in the liver has "gone to sleep". The liver does not *have* to recycle protein, and therefore this particular capacity atrophies through disuse. Nutritionists who claim that the human body needs a certain protein intake consisting of a balance of "essential" amino acids are *correct* in regard to the typical North American adult. All of those ever studied to arrive at this conclusion were meat-eaters or had a typically heavy protein diet, and none of them could have switched over to a minimal protein intake without the usual symptoms of protein deficiency: headaches, malaise, dizzyness and the like. Many individuals who convert too quickly to a meatless diet, even though they continue to consume other sources of protein (like eggs and cheese) find that they develop these symptoms.

And yet the liver can be coaxed to reassume this lost faculty of recycling most or all of the body's protein (in the absence of congenital metabolic disorders). The oxen and horses which pull wagons and ploughs, the elephants that drag or carry heavy loads, do not eat concentrated protein. Their livers are capable of 100% protein recycling. Man's liver is not different from that of these large beasts of burden in terms of protein metabolism. It is just that the faculty is slumbering in man, and must be re-awakened.

The secret is to do so *gradually*. We recommend that any who wish to give up meat and/or reduce their protein intake set up a schedule of at least 18 months over which the conversion can take place. To reduce or cut out meat, do not stop meat altogether at first. Stop eating only *red* meat, but continue to eat fish and fowl for at least 6 months. This is a term longer than suggested in *Seasons of the Spirit*, but we wish to ensure that the period is long enough to suit even those whose systems are slow to react. After six months, drop all meat from the diet, and continue to eat as much eggs, cheese and other concentrated proteins as you wish for about 4 further months. As soon as all meat has been dropped, a series of short fasts may be undertaken. We recommend that these be no longer than three days initially, depending upon the severity of the reaction of the individual. The nature of the fast will depend upon whether the individual is significantly overweight or not. Such fasts should be undertaken every two to three months, but can be more often as determined by the intuition of the individual.

After a certain period of time, possibly after coming off a fast, the individual may find that returning to the previous level of protein intake (eggs, cheese, etc.) gives him a 'full' feeling, as if he had eaten too much food. Alternatively the back of the throat may develop a peculiar, slightly unpleasant sensation when he attempts to eat concentrated protein. Either one of these events is a signal from the body that the level of protein can be reduced. The individual should simply continue to follow the body's own guidelines to end up at the minimum protein intake which is right for him.

Lastly, we should stress that before undertaking any fasting technique, the experimenter should aquaint himself with current writings on the subject. There are many excellent books on fasting, those by Airola being closest to our own views on the matter.

In the "Twelfth Planet", the author Sitchin contends that a group of extra-terrestrials called the Nephilim visited earth a few hundred thousand years ago, and that they literally "made" the current form of human being by genetic engineering. Can you comment on this idea?

The story as recounted in that book is substantially factual, although the time periods do not correspond to reality. The Nephilim were a race of advanced humanoids from a planet outside this sun-system, that landed on and colonized this planet some 300,000 years ago. They were in fact responsible for "making" genetically one of the root races of present humanity — a black-haired, dark-skinned man — by upgrading the genetic composition of "man" as he had previously been on the earth: namely, an upright biped, with little mental activity, largely living as a savage, in tune with the plant and animal life, but not aware of any deeper philosophical or religious notion than a simple fear of the storm and worship of the sun. They had a primitive language, but did not use it much because they were in close psychic contact with each other at all times.

The Nephilim were not "spiritually advanced" beings as you would look at them now. They lacked that universal reverence for life that is one of the essentials for escaping from the necessity for rebirth into the material plane of being. They were, in fact, the *remnant* of a group whose most advanced members had moved on to realms of higher vibration. The Nephilim, then, represented the worst or least evolved fraction of that group. They had passed through their own form of Tribulation, but had failed to make the spiritual leap which entitled their more spiritually evolved brothers to advance.

The descent to earth was planned and promoted by man-

kind's own guides from much higher levels. They manipulated the Nephilim — who were possessed of physical and
mental characteristics which it was desired to infuse into
primitive man's genetic pool — into "giving birth" to a
hybrid form of man — part savage, part Nephilim. The
hybrid was not as evolved physically and mentally as the
Nephilim, but was far superior to his own savage forebears.
The first such hybrid was the individual called *Adam* in
Scriptures, and was ensouled by the entity who later lived
as Jesus of Nazareth.

*Several other sources of verbal transmission claim that not
all of the extra-terrestrial observers have humanity's best
interest at heart. Some contend that certain of the craft
belong to intelligences quite alien or even hostile to us.
What is the truth of the matter? Do we have anything to
fear from these beings?*

This question is a welcome one. We are going to take the
opportunity here to discuss not only the present spacecraft
in the vicinity of the planet, but also those races and
beings which have visited earth in ages past.
We begin with a fundamental truth: that the reality surrounding man is always that which most closely conforms
to his inner state. This applies not only on an individual
basis, but collectively as well. Hence, it must be the case
that certain factors in man's environment now reflect the
negativity, selfishness and rampant materialism of man's
current mode of thinking and behaving. And this is so. The
events now disrupting the planet, the wars and violence in
many parts of the globe, the instabilities in the economic
and political structures — these are all clearly reflective of
man's internal darkness.
Now, as humanity sends out its particular vibration into
space, so it must attract to the planet other beings and
groups which are on a corresponding "frequency", so to

speak. This too does occur. Man's preoccupation with form and materiality for its own sake has attracted the attention of groups whose interest is primarily along these lines. Man's headlong rush to provide himself with horrific weapons of destruction has brought entities to the earth who are particularly responsive to that very negative vibration. Man's emphasis on the unevolved emotions of greed, hate, fear, envy, worry and self-pity have drawn to him those beings whose main "food" consists of these negative states of consciousness.

But in none of these instances are the space-brothers involved. The beings who are drawn by materiality are essentially elemental aetheric forces of low vibration which are the by-products of man's *past* preoccupations with form for its own sake. Those who are attracted by the weaponry are astral in nature, and cannot directly interact with man on the physical plane. The entities who feed on greed, hate and so on are also astral, and hover always within the aura of the planet — seeking out those who indulge in these emotions, prompting them to continue the indulgence, and literally surviving on the vibrations which their victims exude.

But the earth is not solely a planet of darkness. Here and there are pockets of light, love and spiritual purpose. There yet remain a handful of human souls who have managed to keep their attention on the higher truths despite the temptations constantly held out to them life after life.

These, too, have their characteristic vibration. However because their vibration is so much higher and lighter than those of the negative traits previously discussed, it is also far more penetrating and capable of "travelling" much greater distances — not only in the physical three-dimensional universe, but on into higher dimensions and vaster universes as well. It is these higher vibrations that have gone forth as a signal to the other galactic civilizations, and it is only the groups that are on a parallel wavelength that have responded. For this reason, the craft in the earth's region that are able to shift into the material level of manifestation all belong to civilizations far superior to man in the spiritual sense, and with a correspondingly high level of technical achievement. As we have explained in our books, until a civilization achieves a certain pre-determined spiritual level of understanding and development, it is literally not possible for that civilization to advance beyond a particular technical threshold which corresponds to its spiritual state. Man's state of darkness, savagery and materialism has absolutely predetermined that the technical accomplishment attainable by him must remain at the present rather primitive level, until a degree of spirituality is reached which permits a broader understanding.

This is not to say that, in all of the vast regions of creation, there are no other unevolved or primitive civilizations. There are many such, but like that now on the earth, their access to other parts of the universe is restricted by their own spiritual darkness. They too are denied access to the secrets of energy-free space flight. They too have literally confined themselves to their home planets due to the darkness of their minds and hearts.

For the earth, this was not always the case. In times past, there was a necessity that access to the earth be allowed to certain groups who were less than fully evolved in a spiritual sense, but who had learned the secrets of space flight from others. These "others" were in most cases their own brothers who *were* of an evolved nature, but who had separated from the stragglers and passed to higher levels of being, out of the material universe. The so-called "Nephilim" (discussed in another answer in this book) are an example of such a group.

The reason for allowing such access for relatively unevolved groups was primarily to permit them to interbreed with man, or in some other way to upgrade the genetic inheritance of humanity. For, even though these visitors were far less evolved than the present-day galactic observers, nonetheless they had certain genetic characteristics which the Elohim who guide humanity's destiny wished to incorporate into man's genetic pool as it then was. The result was an increase in the size of the head and brain, and the restructuring of the digestive tract.

By comparison, however, the civilizations which now have access to energy-free space flight are only those which are relatively advanced from a spiritual point of view. Indeed, the entire galaxy of which the earth is a part has itself recently advanced spiritually along with all of its component civilizations (it could not be otherwise) and this has required a corresponding increase in the minimum spiritual understanding required to allow access to energy-free space flight. Moreover, the very vibrations which are now flooding the earth to prepare it for the quickening of the Aquarian ideal come originally from the galactic center, being only modified and adapted by the many intermediate levels along the path from that high source to the earth level — and those galactic energies have been released due to the advance of the galactic being.

As to the sources from which come suggestions that some of the physical space-craft belong to unevolved or hostile aliens, we can only advise the reader to search within himself for his own grasp of the truth. We are not allowed to comment unfavorably on other sources of transmission, as we adhere to the Commandments of Freedom.

Can the astrological birth-chart of Jesus be given to us along with a delineation?

The birth-chart of any Avatar or Way-shower is something which has little relevance to the mission and purpose of the incarnation. It is true that all Way-showers who are born through a female channel in the usual way receive an "imprint" or overlay from the positions of the planets at the moment of birth, but in all such cases the soul is powerful enough to completely overcome any pronounced lop-sidedness arising through planetary influence, at least by the start of the "ministry" part of the incarnation. This was the case for the man Jesus, who was freed of the imprint of His birth-chart before he began His 3-year ministry which ended with the Crucifixion.

What is the karmic significance of abortion to the mother, the father and the foetus?

The karmic significance depends, to a great degree, on the motives and reasons behind the action which terminates the life of the foetus.

Birth into earth incarnation is viewed on higher planes as a great opportunity for soul-advancement, for learning, and for spiritual progress. It is also seen by prospective souls as a chance to rejoin loved ones, and to participate in the fulness of physical existence on one of the most beautiful planetary oases in the universe.

Thus from the point of view of the soul that might have come into the world in the aborted foetus, the abortion is merely the shutting of a door, the loss of an opportunity to advance. However, as a general rule, souls who lose the possibility of earth incarnation through deliberate abortion are given another opportunity to incarnate very soon thereafter.

For the woman who arranges or assents to an abortion, the pivotal question is motive. If it is done for strictly selfish reasons, especially when the woman was in a situation in which the child could have been welcomed and cared for, then the killing of the foetus is counted as an act close to murder in the scale of seriousness. The karmic burden arising in such a circumstance is normally met and set aside through the experience of being denied a child when one is wanted . . . either later in the same life, or in some subsequent experience on the earth plane.

At the other end of the scale of motive is the situation in which there are persuasive reasons for terminating the pregnancy, reasons not related to simple selfish desires. For example, where there is a threat to the mother's life or health, or where no family situation exists capable of providing a good early life to the child, then abortion is not taken to be a particularly negative act. *Some* karma stems from it, or course, but it is generally not of a severe nature.

The father of the aborted child is also assessed in strict accordance with his motive, assuming he forces or persuades the mother to have an abortion. It is unnecessary to explain the matter in greater detail.

Is Hilarion aware of the thousands of individuals in almost every country in the world who are presently working towards raising world consciousness and who will eventually make every nation invincible and mankind immortal? How is the work of these individuals and examples of rising world consciousness compatible with Hilarion's warning of the Tribulation and rising negativity in the world?

The warnings which we put forth in our books and other writings are not intended for the thousands who are working to raise the world consciousness. We believe that the *millions* of others who are enmeshed in selfishness, materiality and negative states of mind are also worth rescuing from the juggernaut which is now bearing down on the world. Let us explain this matter more fully.

In man's past, attempts of many kinds have been made to reach out to incarnated individuals, to persuade them to see the truth about the purpose of their lives, to prompt them to take up the cross of service to others. The most significant such attempt was the advent of the Christ Logos, when it lived within the man Jesus. That was an attempt to rescue souls along the *love* vibration. The legacy which Christ left to the world has indeed inspired many millions to follow in His footsteps, and the attempts to do so have allowed many to raise their vibrations so high that no further material incarnations have been required of them.

Another attempt was along a different vibration.

Although it was seen that the love vibration had been successful for a significant proportion of mankind, there nonetheless remained a hardened core of individuals so far gone in selfishness, cruelty and disdain for any law but their own, that they were totally immune to the beautiful example which Christ had set, and the words of great wisdom that He left behind. For these blind ones, the plagues and famines of the last 2000 years were prepared. It was hoped that, where the example of love had failed, perhaps the threat of scarcity or disease would succeed. It must be understood here that the Creative Forces who are responsible for humanity's progress are not above using any means which will rescue souls from the oblivion that awaits those who do not, within the period allowed for the reincarnational scheme, raise their vibrations high enough to be able to move on to loftier spiritual realms along with the rest of their brothers. Many may think that fear and want are, in some manner, unworthy tools to use to prompt men to change. And yet, are they to be rejected when they might succeed in salvaging even a single individual who, by his *own* actions, is dooming himself to being separated from the nobler half of humanity, to regress back to where all uniqueness, all the delightful foibles and traits which make for individuality, are blotted out? For that is precisely what awaits those who do not choose the more spiritual path over the next short period of history. This is not to say that the spiritual *essence* is destroyed, for it is not. But the individualness of the unsuccessful soul must be reabsorbed back into the "sea of spirit", before being "breathed out" again to begin *at the very beginning* to form of itself a unique entity.

The final and most horrendous "tool" to promote spiritualization is one that does not need to be forced upon the earth, for it is merely that which mankind has literally prepared for itself through the centuries of hatred, vengeance, brutality, selfishness and materialism. It is the Tribulation, a period of seven years during which all of the dreadful negativity which man has cast up into the atmosphere of this planet is being allowed to crystallize around him . . . in upheaval, in war and in chaos.

We are not attempting to counteract the wonderful beams of light which the army of Aquarian workers on the earth plane are emitting. We would be pleased beyond our ability to describe if their efforts could reach the hearts and minds of *all* of their brothers, making the Tribulation itself unnecessary. But we see the gathering clouds of war, we know the strains and stresses within the earth's very body, and we perceive clearly the probabilities of eruption and dislocation in the political and economic spheres. Our warnings are an attempt to reach those whose ears have not heard the ominous rumblings, whose eyes are blind to the signs which are all around, whose hearts have not opened to the grander truth regarding the destiny and purpose of the human race.

For these, too, are the children of the Everlasting Father.

Please comment on chiropractic.

This question requires a very complex answer, one which we do not wish to offer in its totality in this publication. However, we will sketch a general approach to the art of Chiropractic which will allow the reader to understand how we view the technique from this level. The basic idea which underlies the development of Chiropractic is that the condition of the spine is a principal determinative for the general health of the body. In a very real sense, that is correct. The spine is the passage along which all of the major energies of the body flow: not only those associated with the physical vehicle, but those which move in the astral and aetheric bodies as well. The chakras or wheels of aetheric energy in the aetheric body are all connected to a center line along the back of that body — corresponding to the spine in location.

Thus it happens that any major disruptions in the smooth flow of energy along the spinal chord, or any physical abnormality or blockage, can greatly affect the body in any number of critical ways.

The only error that is occasionally made by chiropractors is to assume that they can, with their manipulations, cure in a permanent way all problems that stem from spinal irregularities. In many instances, however, the spine is congenitally weak in certain regions, due to karmic causes, while in others the individual has a habit of thought which creates what are called thought-forms capable of bringing about serious structural and functional disorders in the spine and then in other related parts of the body.

Please suggest a method of neutralizing feelings of anger and irritation toward others.

The way to approach the matter of over-coming such negative emotionalism is simple to state, but difficult to put into practice for most souls who have little control over their emotional states. The way to proceed is to *love* those for whom anger or irritation might be felt. Where love is, no negative emotions can exist.

This simple precept requires that the individual understand that the ability to love *is under the command of his will*. Too many people are unaware that they are fully capable of directing their love and affection toward *any* soul, animal or entity whatever, and that they are not simply at the whim of infatuation, nor do they require some mysterious "chemistry" or natural attraction before they can feel affection. The heart chakra was meant to be an obedient instrument of the self, just as the various head centers were meant to be.

We wish to suggest a simple exercise which will demonstrate that a feeling of love *can* be projected toward any being, regardless of whether affection had previously been felt for that being. First, picture in your mind the person for whom you have the most love and affection at the moment. Allow yourself to feel an outrush of love for that soul, remembering that he/she is a fragment of God and fully deserving of all the love you can generate. Next, hold that feeling of love, that outrush of affection, and sustain it — while you allow the picture of the person to fade away and be replaced by another person of whom you are also quite fond. Keep the emotion of love flowing. It *is* possible to do this with some practice.

Next, while still keeping the affectional feeling in your heart, replace the second person with someone who is merely an acquaintance, for whom you normally do not have any emotional feeling, either good or bad.

Finally — and remember that you *can* do this — replace that acquaintance with someone whom you normally dislike, while still beaming out love and affection toward him/her.

Do not feel that, by doing this, you are placing yourself at a disadvantage with respect to that person. You may be tempted to think that, if you love that enemy while he remains bitter against you, he may be able to harm you in some way. Nothing could be further from the truth. Indeed, by the very act of loving that former enemy, you are setting up energy patterns which actually *prevent* that enemy from doing you any injury. Few people realize that one's enemy is *strengthened* by one's hatred, but quite disarmed and confused by love. If you hate your enemy, you feed him negative energy which he can use to keep up his end of the battle. But if you send him only affection and love, his own enmity toward you perishes for lack of being "fed".

There are other techniques to use, such as visualizing a magenta color around the heart chakra, meditating on the true meaning of love, and praying to the Christ to teach you to feel love for all. Any who are drawn to these other techniques should of course follow their intuition. However, we have provided a straightforward mental and emotional technique that many readers of this publication, because of their fifth ray emphasis, will be able to use profitably in their search for perfection.

Hal Lindsey, in "There's a New World Coming", contends that those who are into occultism, astrology and such are "in league with the devil", and implies that they are anti-Christian. Yet in your books you show how these esoteric teachings are spiritualizing forces for humanity. Firstly, why do traditionalist Christians dislike occultism? Secondly, do you see any process of conversion or reconciliation which will bring the religious fundamentalists to a broader view of reality?

The questions are complex, for they require a dissertation on the purpose and history of the Christian tradition during the Piscean Age. The matter is even more involved, because certain of the darker forces are allowed to work through both the traditional religious sources and the occult sources in order to promote division, strife and mistrust between these two groups.

The answer to the first question is that the spokesmen for traditional Christianity are basing their views on ignorance and on the handed-down dogmas of the church. No one who has seriously looked into the mystery teachings could possibly contend that they hold anything but the greatest promise for redemption and soul-evolution for man. Indeed, *all* of the great way-showers on this planet, including Jesus of Nazareth, were occultists and adepts of great accomplishment. When Jesus calmed the storm, walked on water or healed the sick with a simple touch, He was not calling upon some mysterious God to perform miracles for Him; He was not implementing any process which was not an integral part of the functioning of the universe if properly understood. He was simply using the talents and training which He had attained during the years when He travelled to other cultures to learn at the feet of the sages then on the earth plane. These sages showed Him how to employ the powers of visualization, will and the spoken word, in order to make His environment conform to His wishes.

Many times He said that what He did, any other man

could also do. This statement was based on His certain knowledge that the techniques of Mastership were available to all who were willing diligently to follow the Path of Attainment.

Thus, it happens that the very man who provided the teachings upon which the Christian Church is founded was Himself one of the greatest occultists and adepts that ever walked the earth.

As to the matter of church dogma, any who care to study the true history of the Christian Church from unbiased sources will quickly learn that the church of Rome was, during many parts of its history, quite favorably disposed towards occultism. Many popes had their own personal astrologers, whose advice they followed. Even in the present day, the Vatican possesses the most complete and diversified library on esoterism and the occult in the world.

Thus, those of fundamentalist persuasion, ignorant of the real truth behind the mystery tradition, basing their views largely on misinterpretations of biblical passages that have suffered much in translation and (in some cases) been deliberately changed from the original, and occasionally wishing to discredit a philosophy which they see as competing with Christianity for the minds and hearts of human souls, have quite understandably adopted a crusader-like stance toward all that smacks of the occult.

There is also a residue of the old witch-hunting mentality in all who are deeply imbued with certain Scriptural passages which deal with the devil as a personification of evil, who can tempt souls from the true path. Of course, there is indeed an entity who corresponds to the chief of the fallen angels, but the notion that he can have any access to souls whose eyes remain fixed on the light is completely false.

As to the second question, that related to the process of reconciliation, we do of course envision a time on the earth when all men will be harmonious in their views of the reality of God, the purpose of life, and the way to achieve mastership of the problems which physical incarnation poses. This reconciliation will take time, however, for man must devise his own future, and each living soul must decide for himself what he will think. Nonetheless, it is likely that many of the manifestations upon the earth over the next few decades will be beyond the capacity of any traditional religion to fully explain. The mass sightings of craft flown by the galactic observers, the spontaneous manifestation of clairvoyance in children and many adults who have purified themselves physically and emotionally, and the various symbols which will appear in the sky — many known only to occultists — will squarely challenge the old way of thinking.

The categories of thought which characterized the Piscean Age are inadequate to explain the wonders of the Age of Light soon to dawn. In their place, a new philosophy of love, expansion and reconciliation will have to evolve. The key to finding joy and fulfillment during the wondrous time of rebirthing for man, is to be an active part of the search for a new vessel into which the waters of love, light, spirituality and service can be poured. Those who cling stubbornly to the old categories and prejudices will find only confusion, doubt and a darkness of understanding.

May the fountains of glory from the highest levels pour out their gift of light and love upon this planet at last! The night of sorrows is drawing, finally, to an end.

OM MANI PADME HUM

Is the name Hilarion suggestive of the "angel of proclamation" concept, that is, announcing a coming event with a trumpet?

The significance of names involves influences and factors that are far too complicated to explain at the level of this transmission. The name of each soul on the earth plane is filled with meaning, indeed with meanings that are found on many levels. If the source of this question wishes to seek a more comprehensive answer to any question regarding the meaning of a name, we suggest that he attain it through meditation and prayer. Only in this way can the soul glimpse certain truths that cannot be expressed verbally.

Will the Tribulation end the materialistic philosophy forever?

In order to answer this question properly, we must first draw a distinction between "materialism" and "working with form". It is part of man's experience on the earth plane to learn how to deal with form in a creative way. He builds buildings, constructs machines, works through and learns about his own body, creates works of sculpture, painting and so on. These activities are all part of his learning process — a process that requires him to deal with and manipulate material matter by changing its *form*. It is not this process which leads to negative results. Indeed, the plan for humanity calls for human souls to become masters at the art of creating in form, not only by carrying out physical operations on matter, but literally by learning how to do this by the power of thought alone.

The problem arises when man begins to think that matter is *all there is*, that form is an end in itself, and that material objects are desirable in and for themselves. In such a conclusion, man forgets that he is upon the earth plane merely to *learn* about matter and form, not to form an attachment to it that can stand in the way of spiritual progress. It is this *attachment* to matter (in its many varied forms) which constitutes materialism in our definition of the term.

The question is whether the Tribulation will end the materialistic philosophy. What we would like to point out is that the Tribulation is the *result* of the materialistic philosophy, in large measure. It has not been decreed as a punishment for man, nor as a means of jolting him out of his current mode of thinking. The Tribulation merely *is*, and has been created by the very energies which the materialistic mode of behavior spawns.

Regardless of this point, however, it *is* likely that the experience of the Tribulation upon the earth will encourage millions of souls to rethink their philosophies, and to see that matter and form are merely tools for learning. Once this thought has become implanted, it is not likely that the errors of the current world-view of man will be repeated.

Can you discuss the assassination attempt on the Pope? What spiritual purpose was served by this dreadful act?

Whenever any soul wishes to serve the race in a prominent way, it may be selected for a leading role in earth life. For example, a soul may be asked to volunteer to live a life such that there is a strong possibility that the personality will become the President of the United States. This cannot be seen absolutely at the time of birth, since the future is always in a state of flux. However, certain probabilities can be forseen, and certain individuals can be manipulated into positions where they are likely candidates for that office.

Whenever a soul agrees to this kind of potential role, it must also agree that, if decided by humanity's guides, the physical body may be damaged or even killed if the progress of the race can be furthered through such a circumstance. The case of John Kennedy is a good illustration. The soul was approached and asked if it would agree to such a sacrifice life, and it was pointed out that it might well be necessary to take him out of earth life through assassination if he won the election of 1960. The soul agreed, out of the highest and noblest motives, to serve his brothers in this way, and the rest is history.

One might well wonder what good end *was* served by taking Kennedy in 1963. Briefly, the good that came of it occurred in the *hearts* of Americans. The grief united the country as no earlier loss had ever done, and the bonds which were then established — bonds of commiseration and love — have remained intact to the present. There were other considerations leading to the guides' decision to remove Kennedy at that time, relating to world events, but the main purpose was to unite America.

It will now be clear that the sacrifice life being lived by the Pope would also call for him to agree to the possibility of damage to the physical body. The purpose served here was to unite the Christian community of the world in concern, hope and prayer, and thus weld it into a powerful instrument for spirituality on the earth. Another purpose was to demonstrate in graphic terms to all men who retain a shred of moral decency how base the earth has become. It is this baseness that man *must* see, if he is to realize that everyone has, to a greater or lesser extent, some echo of this violence and treachery within him. For until man can see clearly his own inner state, there will never be any inducement for him to purify himself.

In recent "space movies", such as Star Wars and others, a number of the alien animals and settings look curiously earth-like. Can you comment upon the similarities and disparities between the life-forms and environments on other planets as compared with the earth?

The question opens a vast area for discussion. There are many planets that are so alien by comparison to earth, that the forms and beings there would not even be recognized by earth eyes as having any essence at all. Clouds which talk, energy balls that can manifest in any form whatever — these life patterns are alien beyond any description in earth language. Even some of the most imaginative science fiction writers have not glimpsed the wealth of variation and strangeness which exists within the created worlds.

But there are planets where the forms known on the earth are found. Many species located here are also on these other planets, in practically the identical form. In fact if such forms were to be transplanted from the other planets to the earth, the corresponding species could even mate and produce offspring. This should not seem too strange, however, since in many cases (particularly with mammals) that is precisely how the species arrived on earth in the first place.

We should point out that many species known on the earth are considered to be very adaptable forms, and excellent for transplanting from one sun-system to another. For example, the cat family represents an extremely adaptive form, one which can get along in the most variegated circumstances. It can learn to eat food of many kinds — including flesh — and can adopt habits which protect it against almost any natural predator. It can adapt to extreme heat and extreme cold. Its reflexes are very quick. The fastest land animal on the earth belongs to the cat family.

When a new planet is being considered for "seeding" with a number of life-forms, the cat family is invariably studied as a possiblity.

As to environments, we will restrict ourselves to those planets which are at the material or physical level of vibration, and thus equivalent to the earth. In general, such planets are under conditions which compare well with those on the earth. However, few of them have as much water on the surface, and most are somewhat hotter and dryer. The atmospheres range in oxygen content, depending upon the vegetation that is present. There are, however, many planets on whose surface man from this earth could, with a bit of effort, survive quite well.

That is as much as we can offer in answer to such a general question.

101

What is the future for marriage, family and community living?

The future, as we have pointed out, is in a state of flux. In answering this question we can only provide an overview of the most likely probabilities as seen at the time of this writing. We emphasize that man makes his own future — *with his thought.* By means of projecting forward certain expectations, hopes and fears, mankind literally creates the details of that which is to come. When we, in our writings, set forth certain glimpses of the future on this planet, we are in part attempting to influence the direction of development in the most spiritual sense, and in part we are indicating that which appears from our instruments to be the most likely actual direction. We will explain this concept further.

There are many sources which speak through psychics and telepaths and which are eager to sketch the likelihoods of future possibilities in response to questions. We stress that *all* such sources, including ourselves, are subject to the limitations that arise naturally from the fact that man has been given the gift of free will. This means that no entity at any plane can actually say for certain what direction mankind as a whole will choose. Since we and all such sources are under this severe limitation, we (and they) will often take the opportunity of a future-oriented question to set forth a particularly desirable picture from a spiritual point of view, thereby creating a thought-form in a number of minds, in the hope that such reinforcement of our own picture will help to bring the reality of it into being.

Do not feel that we are in any sense "cheating" by doing so. We are merely attempting to help steer the race in the direction of evolution in yet another way. We work and strive always to uplift our brothers in incarnation — through direct thought-influence, through writings of this nature, and through other means too complex to be described in earth language. Why should we not use this additional way of reaching out a helping hand to our brothers?

Turning now to the question regarding the future of marriage, the family and community living, we will state first that the direction is very much up to the collective desires of the race. However, there are certain facts which we will present here, and which allow the most likely direction to be at least glimpsed. We have pointed out many times in our writings that one of the tasks with which mankind has wrestled was the development of a sense of individuality and self-worth. This required that individuals be separated from each other in their self-conceptions, and that the original tendency of men to see themselves as merely fragments of the entire racial group be overcome. Now man is at the beginning of the trek back to a feeling of belonging to a unified group. But progress in this direction must not be made by sacrificing all the gains that have been won in terms of self-image and the development of the lovable quirks and foibles of billions of individuals. No, the reunification must come about not through dissolving individuals in an amorphous mass, but through the spread of *love* among all members of the human family. By so doing, the uniqueness and individuality of the component souls can be preserved, as was intended from the beginning.

Now, if man is to preserve the uniqueness and the *differences* between individual souls, there is likely to be a limit to the degree to which men can live in close association with each other, at least in the initial phases of the New Age. Man has grown used to having his own space, and to the enjoyment of solitary places. Many souls have lived lives of separation from their fellows, as hermits, as monks, as recluses. And in most such cases these individuals have, through their solitary experiences, grown closer to their real essence and to God. For God speaks to man in the silence of his own heart, and that heart-silence is not always easy to discover in the rush and tumult of a busy life constantly distracted by the need to attend to the demands of others.

Thus, man is a mixture — a strange paradox. He needs his time alone, and yet he needs the support and contact of others. It is likely then, that while somewhat greater "community of living" will be a part of the New Age about to dawn, this probably will not be taken to the extent where humans are totally immersed in mutual contact. All souls feel the need for isolation and quiet thought at times, and any community which does not allow for these moments of tranquility and separation will not be feeding all the needs of the soul.

As to the family, we doubt whether this pattern of living will be tossed aside in the early stages of the new phase of civilization about to be commenced. Indeed, it is the family unit that has provided the initial kernel from which the concept of community living has grown. The family was the first community, as those who have studied anthropology will understand, and as such — with its built-in encouragement to love and care for each other, with its blood-ties and natural affinities — it will in all probability remain the best example of a loving, caring, nurturing "community" in which physical, mental, emotional and spiritual needs are tended.

With reference to marriage, there has always been intended for man the close mating or pairing which society has formalized into the institution of marriage. Marriage in terms of its rigorous *form* may well change and evolve through the decades to come, but the idea that two souls on the earth reserve their most intimate love for *each other* is rooted so deeply in the history and the very essence of the human race, that we see no likelihood that it will soon be replaced.

Please explain how Christ was able to forgive sins and heal people when there was another law which stated that "as you sow, so shall you reap".

The experiences of the Christ do not fit fully within the general scheme of the cosmic laws, because the Christ was literally a part of the Highest Creator and as such, could suspend or annul any of those laws. It is true that the expression, "as you sow, so shall you reap" conveys the truth of the karmic requirement decreed from the very beginning of manifestation, and this law still continues in force throughout the created worlds. However, the Christ decided to lift the karmic burdens from the shoulders of certain individuals, in order to demonstrate that such lifting of karma was possible. Indeed, as we have explained in our writings, it is always possible for a given quantum of karma to be removed and assumed by another entity. In the case of the Christ, He Himself assumed whatever karma remained and was at the root of the illness or suffering of the individual who was healed and forgiven.

A further comment, however, is in order in regard to the "forgiveness of sins". We have explained in other writings that, in God's eyes, there is no guilt and no sin. His love for all beings and entities is so vast that there is no room for reproof, accusation or condemnation. *God does not condemn.* It is *man* that judges and condemns himself, for all men know within the core of their being what constitutes holy and evolved action. And each man writes in his own record-sheet the details of the acts which are against the laws of creation, love and spirituality. The karma is automatic, arising immediately as a consequence of any negative action; and just as automatic is the necessity that any karma of this nature must at some time be set aside through suffering. Usually the suffering is on the part of the one responsible for the original action, but occasionally, as in the instances of healing by Christ, the burden is assumed by another being.

Did man evolve from lower life-forms or did God make man in finished form?

The question assumes that man is a life-form that either had to evolve from an initial more primitive species, or was made fully manifest in his present form. Neither of these

105

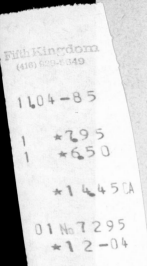

concepts expresses the full truth of the matter.

In order to explain, we must sketch the theory of *life-streams*, so that the reader will grasp the nature of the energies and categories that this question evokes. Mankind is a single life-stream which has had many earlier experiences in forms other than human, but which is now concentrating on the lessons which the human form can teach. For example, the life-stream which is now humanity on this planet has undergone a mineral manifestation, one in the vegetable kingdom, and another as an animal genus including a number of species. However these more elementary learning phases are now in the past, the lessons have been mastered, and the karma arising from the earlier manifestations has been set aside.

Each life-stream, as we point out in *Other Kingdoms*, is "breathed forth" from the sea of spirit, sometimes called the "Body of God", to begin its sequence of life-form experiences. These follow normally in the order: air, mineral, vegetable, animal, man. It is important to realize that the *essence* of the life-stream exists apart from any dependence upon any given *form*, whether animal, mineral, man or whatever. The essence is never lost and has neither a beginning nor an end — in the sense that it comes from the Father and ultimately returns to Him. The forms which any life-stream inhabits are merely tools for learning and are not to be considered a special or unique characteristic of the life-stream.

Now, the human form which man now uses for learning on the earth plane has been the preferred form for only some ten million years — a period much shorter than the animal phase was, for example, and vastly shorter than the mineral, at least as man now measures time. But length of time is not the most significant factor. What is important is the rapidity of the learning that any particular phase can offer to the life-stream. Generally speaking, the phase of man allows much faster assimilation of important lessons, whereas the mineral and vegetable phases are more difficult to learn through and require more time.

The reason for explaining the background to this question is now plain: the form which this life-stream is currently using, being merely one of a series of forms, is not as important as the realization that the *essence* of man is the life-stream as a whole. Having stated that, however, we do wish to give some understanding of the process through which the current model of man was developed for the life-stream. When the life-stream began its phase as man, it could not immediately inhabit a complex, rational and sensitive vehicle such as the current physical body which humanity uses. The previous experiences of the life-stream had not prepared it to think consciously or to feel at the depth which is now common. Only the *physical* sensations were to some extent familiar. Therefore, there had to be a long period of acclimatization to the basic pattern of man, and this had to take place without any profound experience of rational thought or emotional sensitivity. These latter characteristics, it was known, would develop slowly with the passage of time and the accumulation of experience. Hence, the first manifestation of this life-stream as man on the earth utilized an aetheric form (as it would now be considered), of the general configuration of man, but with only a single eye. The fragments of the life-stream inhabiting these creatures were not thinking, rational entities, but rather functioned largely upon the psychic levels to keep in tune with each other. Indeed, there was little concept of separateness as between the different units, since they all felt still that they were essentially one entity, namely the life-stream itself. In order to instill a sense of individuality, many adventures and phases had to be experienced. Many of these are hinted at in the material which Edgar Cayce brought through psychically. Still other experiences were intended to contribute to man an emotional/affectional nature, and then later phases were planned so that the spark of rationality and intellect could be fanned into flame. We have not the space required to detail all of these fascinating adventures as they actually happened. Soon, however, the true records of the human race will be discovered, and they will make plain what we have here only hinted at.

Finally we may address the original question: how man attained his present life-form. The form has gone through many changes, as it adapted to the advances of intellect and emotion which the life-stream was mastering. However, these changes would never have arisen merely through Darwinian "natural selection" and the "survival of the fittest". In a world where physical prowess determined aptitude for mere physical survival, the Darwinian process would have allowed the strongest and more brutish types to predominate, and the genetic inheritance from these individuals would not have been one that would have allowed the flowering of the intellect or the blossoming of the emotional nature.

In order to permit these special adaptations, certain additional strains of "man" were fed into the genetic pool at various times in man's history. When it was necessary to give man a greater capacity for rational and abstract thought, a strain of human from a particular sun-system was imported and mixed genetically with man as he then was on this planet. When an increase in emotional sensitivity was to be brought into manifestation, another genetic strain was brought, and so on.

We understand that what we have set out above will not sit well with many who wish to take the words of Genesis literally, namely that God made man in His image. However, we have explained elsewhere that the underlying occult meaning of this phrase is that man possesses the *Triangle of Being*, i.e. the capacity for physical, emotional and mental experience, thus manifesting at his own level the same categories as are found in the Highest Creator, represented as God the Father, the Christ, and the Holy Ghost. At a simpler level, this phrase in Genesis should be read in the *plural* (as it is in the original Hebrew: Elohim), that the *gods* made man in their image. This part of the scriptures, as so many others, was meant to be true at several levels simultaneously. Hence, in addition to the meaning relating to the Triangle of Being, there is also the interpretation according to which the "gods", i.e. certain advanced humanoids from another star-system, using techniques of genetic engineering, literally "made" a new and more advanced life-form for the human life-stream to work through, the new form being one very close to their own *image* because certain of their genetic characteristics were transplanted into the human stock as it then was.

We have attempted here to detail some of the vast concepts behind the simple query as to man's current form. However, we have no wish to detract from the fundamental and eternal notion that "man" stems from God ultimately, and that in the last analysis it is God who has made not only man, but everything that is manifest in Creation. He makes each life-stream; He projects the environment for that stream to inhabit; and — through lesser beings to whom He has entrusted the task and given the great privilege of creating life-forms — He brings into being the perfect vehicles at just the right times to allow the life-stream to progress spiritually at the fastest rate.

Please expand upon the apparent difference between Hal Lindsey's views of occultism and that of Hilarion. Lindsey states that those who mix occultisms in any way with the teachings of the Bible and Christianity will perish.

Do not consider this notion on the part of that author to be a flaw in his work. There is a level of meaning to that statement which can be looked on as correct, namely that those who try to mix the *darker* side of occultism with Christianity are in trouble. Mr Lindsey has a particularly strong repugnance for the black arts in this life because of certain past experiences, and in view of this his opposition is understandable. However the seeker after the highest wisdom must realize that God does not place any thing or technique on the earth as something inherently evil. It is only *man* that perverts to evil uses that which God has presented to him as essentially neutral — to be used for good or ill as *man* chooses. Unfortunately, man has throughout many centuries chosen to use the occult powers inherent in the mind for his own selfish goals, harming others, causing illness and even death, and generally bringing sorrow and destruction to this planet. It is this improper use of God's gifts which that author dislikes, and rightly so. He is not aware, however, that Christ Himself was one of the greatest adepts and occultists that ever lived and walked the earth, and that He was merely using His great understanding of God's laws to carry out the acts that are reported in the Scriptures as "miracles". We do not say that no miracles were performed, but rather that *all of life is a miracle* — that miracle of God's love for man, the miracle of existence itself.

We have received many questions asking about the expected changes in various areas of the world over the next decades, the magnetic pole shift, the extent of destruction during the Tribulation, etc. Rather than submit each such question, we have asked for a general comment on these requests for "prophecy".

We are aware that many souls wish to be reassured against what they see as the threat of danger during the upheavals that are inevitable over the coming few years. We sympathize with those who are concerned for themselves and their loved ones; however there is something which needs to be emphasized for such souls, for they have not grasped one of the most important of the cosmic laws which govern the patterns of life on the earth. It is this: that nothing is left to chance where the saving of souls is concerned. All those who have recognized in these writings a truth which they can make their own are, to a greater or lesser extent, "on the Path". And as such, these individuals are considered important to the general rescue operation that will be launched in a very short time. Therefore, there is no possibility that the guides and teachers who control the development of earth events would allow mere chance to stand in the way of making full use of the knowledge which these souls have attained. The best way to put the matter is this: each person will be in the right place at the right time, and there is no need to worry about whether this area will be safe, or whether to remove one's family to higher ground, etc. None who are seekers will be left in the path of the juggernaut which is bearing down upon the earth. All will be removed to a place of safety to await the opportunity to rebuild the earth. Simply wait and watch. Read the signs; do as your guides and intuition tell you; and *trust* that God has all things in His hand. Remember the biblical comparison. Did not Christ point to the lillies of the field and chide those who gave too much thought for the future, who worried about that which is to come? Surely if God can so clothe the flowers of the field, He will look after those who are about His business.

As to the predictions which we have given in our books, close inspection will reveal that they are principally elaborations of prophecies which are found in scriptures. Beyond these there is little use in investigating. Only the Biblical predictions are such that they *must* be seen to manifest. Anything beyond that represents merely *probability* seen at the time of the question. Even the great and gifted Edgar Cayce made certain prognostications which were not fulfilled. So it will be with some of the predictive material that has been given through this and other sources. The future is definitely in a state of flux; it depends always upon the collective mind of man, for it is *man* that makes his own reality. That, after all, is one of the cosmic mechanisms which was to ensure that humanity would come finally to see its own true essence. If we were able at this point in time to see clearly an unavoidable destiny with no possibility of alteration, then where would man find his free will, and what purpose would earth existence serve? There must always be the possibility that man can change and escape the future that he appears now to have set himself. Indeed, it is the hope of any spiritual source that, by predicting the most difficult of the possible paths, mankind can be induced to change for the better, and thus avoid the worst that has been forseen.

Is there an occult or hidden significance to the death of Bobby Sands? Is there any positive effect of a suicide of this kind? (Bobby Sands was an I.R.A. member convicted and jailed in Northern Ireland. He died after a protracted fast.)

The taking of one's own life is a complex matter from a spiritual point of view. The most important question to be asked is, what was the *motive* of the suicide? If the motive was purely a selfish one — as in those cases where suicide is chosen as a means of ending the pain of existence or to punish someone else — then it is one of the basest acts possible. However, where the one ending his own life does so in an attempt to help or save the life of another, then it is looked on as a supreme act of love and bravery. There is a world of difference between the person who casts his life aside because he wishes no longer to live, and the person who dies while struggling to rescue another human being on a battlefield or in a burning house.

In the case of Sands, we are not permitted to reveal what was in his mind in terms of motivation, but we can say that through this act Sands raised his own vibrations. To a large extent the self-destruction was a form of compensation for the violence and death of which he had been guilty in this life.

Remember that all such cases, i.e. the ones that come to the attention of the public through the media, usually have hidden elements far beyond the simple story as it is directly reported. For example, one of the effects of Sands' death was to put the Irish nation to a test of self-control, to see how deeply rooted the self-hatred had become. The incentive to violence within Ireland immediately after Sands' death was the greatest that it had been for a long time. If the nation — including both parts — can keep the lid on the violence even under this extreme test, then the guides of that country will conclude that the darkness is perhaps not so widespread as they had feared.

This brings up an interesting point. Many might think that a country's guides ought to know intimately the state of affairs within it. However that is not true, any more than it is true that a person's own guides must know intimately what stage he has reached. The very reason for many of the tests and trials that are endured on the earth plane is precisely to allow the guides and teachers at higher planes to assess accurately the progress that has been made or the ground that has been lost.

How can we convince our children to eat proper food?

The answer to this question depends very much upon the nature of the child. It is the case that some children *must* learn from their own experience, and no amount of persuasion or force will make them do something they do not wish to do. There are others who are very open to the words and examples of their elders, simply because they came into the earth with a determination to pick up as much as possible from those who are older. The matter must be judged on the basis of the reaction of the child. The best answer we can give in a general way is, do not coerce any child to do something he refuses. Offer a good example in all things, not only diet, and be willing to explain the reasons for your choices whenever the child asks. But apart from this, there is little that can be done. It is the right of the parents, of course, to decide what kinds of food shall be consumed in their home, and it is justifiable to expect and require the child to conform to these guidelines. However, the complexity of life today, and the interchange of influence from other children and society as a whole, are such that it would be impractical to force an unwilling child to adopt dietary habits which he dislikes and to adhere to them in all circumstances, even while away from the home. Such a situation would probably turn the child into a "cheater", and this would do damage to his self-image — probably more serious damage than the eating of sugar or meat would do.

We would also remind many parents for whom this question is a concern that few of them have adhered to their present dietary restrictions from childhood. In most cases, the person now asking this question has followed a restrictive diet only for a matter of years, before which he or she likely indulged in all of the same 'junk foods', meat, etc., which they now wish to deny their own children. And yet, they — the parents — survived that onslaught of deleterious foods. It is likely that their children will do the same. The human body has near-miraculous powers of recovery and the ability to throw off vast quantities of poisons and toxins that are ingested. Even after forty or fifty years of consuming harmful foods there is a strong likelihood (in the absence of congenital weakness) that the body can be restored to the peak of health merely by undergoing fasts and a restricted diet for about two years.

Above all, treat your children with love, not force. The little ones respond far better to affection than to coercion. Is it not wise to approach the matter as God Himself approaches man? . . . namely to allow man to do as he pleases, to teach the truth and set examples of right-living (through His way-showers), and to know ultimately that experience is the best teacher through the law of cause and effect. It is a fact that more children have turned away from candy through being allowed once to indulge to the point where they made themselves sick, than through having been commanded to refrain.

"Om Mani Padme Hum" — if directed to a person or thing, will it have any effect?

The expression given is a "Holy Breath", as we have pointed out previously. As such it is primarily useful to call down to *oneself* the higher vibrations that exist on the upper planes of manifestation. However, there is a technique by which these higher energies can be first drawn to oneself, then redirected to another. This is accomplished by first visualizing the other person within one's own aura, as if the two were together in the same energy field, and *then* repeating "Om Mani Padme Hum" three times. While this is being said, the operator should visualize both himself and the other person as being flooded with a magenta light.

Is the exposure of the eyes to sunlight a valid technique for self-improvement? Did Jesus teach this?

The exposure of the eyes to direct sunlight is primarily a means of absorbing *energy*, and not so much a technique for self-improvement. Indeed, until a person has achieved a certain degree of purity and thus "improvement", he will be unable safely to allow the light of the sun to fall directly upon the retina. Let us be more specific. The general state of physical bodies in the present day is such that considerable damage would be done to the retina if it were exposed to direct sunlight for more than a few seconds at most. This is because the vibrations of the average body are so coarse and elementary that the much higher vibration inherent in the sun's light would not match the body's rate, and this mismatch would give rise to much stress and damage. However, for those who have carefully cleansed their bodies and their thoughts of the poisons — both physical and mental — which are rampant in the world today, the technique of direct energy absorption from the sun is possible. We would recommend that no one undertake such a technique until he has been a total vegetarian for at least one full year. Also, of course, much study of spiritual things should also be undertaken, and a form of meditation, prayer or contemplation should have become a part of the daily activities. When the seeker feels ready to begin, he should first make a 'shield' for himself. The shield consists of a piece of black paper or cardboard, with two pin pricks spaced apart the distance between the eyes. On a clear day, hold the shield up over the eyes and adjust it until the pin pricks allow the sun's light into the open eyes. Do not look directly at the light coming through the shield. Instead, look off to one side or the other, so that the eyes' focus is not directly on the light. Allow an exposure no longer than ten seconds at first. After a week the exposure may gradually be lengthened up to one minute. The next stage is to *gradually* (we stress this) widen the small holes in the shield by using nails of gradually increasing diameter. Take a full month or even two to widen the holes.

We stress that the seeker must at all times monitor himself carefully. The body will signal to him when the degree of exposure is more than it can take. This it will do by experiencing lingering after-images, or some other form of impairment of vision. If and when this happens, suspend the experiments for a week. Then gradually begin again. If the symptoms reappear, the body was not ready for this technique, and another six months of purification should be undertaken before another attempt is made to begin the technique.

Above all, do not rush into this technique. We do not wish to see over-zealous seekers do damage to their eyes by rushing head-long into an experience for which their bodies are not ready.

As to whether the Master taught this means of absorbing energy, we can say that He taught much to his private circle of disciples that was not conveyed to the masses. He did touch on this matter of energy from the sun through the eyes, but did not recommend that any should begin to follow it, due to the fact that all men then, including His disciples, were still consuming meat (though mainly fish).

Must one belong to communes or the like to be on the spiritual path?

The question of the best way to achieve progress on the path is a highly individual one. There are those who can make headway against their own base natures only by associating themselves with others in a communal form of living. There are others whose individuality is so strong that a constant intermingling with others would merely distract their energies, and leave little strength to get on with the path of self-discipline. Each soul must judge the matter for himself.

In answer to the specific question, it is certainly *not* a prerequisite to spiritual progress to belong to a commune or similar group. Indeed, those who have in ages past chosen the opposite direction — to isolate themselves and live as a hermit — have in many cases moved ahead faster than can be done in a group-setting. This is not to say that isolation from one's fellows is a preferred method, since this too leads to difficulties of another sort (as we have pointed out elsewhere). What we are saying is that there is much to be learned and absorbed in *any* walk of life by one whose spiritual eyes are open, including both extremes we have just mentioned.

Please comment on 1 Timothy 4: 1—5:

"Now the spirit expressly says that in latter times some will depart from the faith by giving heed to deceitful spirits and doctrines of demons, through the pretensions of liars whose consciences are seared, who forbid marriage and enjoin abstinence from foods which God created to be received with thanksgiving by those who believe and know the truth. For everything created by God is good, and nothing is to be rejected if it is received with thanksgiving; for then it is consecrated by the word of God and prayer."

This quotation has many times been utilized to justify the eating of materials which are in fact forbidden in other parts of the Scriptures. For example, it is found in 1st Genesis that God has given man the fruit and nuts produced by trees, stating that "this shall be to you as meat". The implication is that the produce from the trees is intended to be used *instead* of flesh-meat, and it is this philosophy which we have attempted to explain in our writings.

The key part of the quotation here is the expression "food which God created to be received...". What the reader must decide is what constitutes *food* within the meaning intended. For example, if you were to visit a tribe of cannibals, sit down to a meal, and then discover just as you were about to tuck in that the main dish consisted of the losers in the most recent tribal skirmish, you would probably object to the fare as unsuitable. Then, if your host should point to 1 Timothy and quote the material given above, urging that "everything created by God is good, and nothing is to be rejected if it is received with thanksgiving", how would you answer? Would you accept the scriptural authority and start eating the bodies of your brothers? Of course not. The point here is that you must decide for yourself what are the foods which were *intended* for man. Our argument is that the race has unthinkingly fallen into the habit of eating the cadavers of innocent animals, and that neither God nor any other entity ever intended man to partake of so grisly a feast.

Would you please explain the meaning of the Beast with ten horns and seven heads, referred to in Revelations, which will be allowed to exercise authority for 42 months.

This expression has meaning at many levels, as do all of the symbolic concepts contained in the Book of Revelations. The meaning at the practical or physical level is as stated by Lindsey in his writings, namely the European community of nations. As to the more subtle levels of significance, the most important of these is that of the dark patches within individual human souls, i.e. the fragments which were taken into the soul at the time of the Gift of Permanence which we have discussed in our book on the Dark Brotherhood. It is among the great challenges for man to overcome his own "Beast" within, and to transmute that darkness into light while still retaining its power. Many have made great strides in this endeavor, while others have allowed the blackness to swallow up what illumination they might originally have had. All is up to the free will choice of the individual. The darkness too has its allure, even as has the light. The attractiveness of darkness is its emphasis on pleasure and on the aggrandizement of the self, whereas the appeal of the light lies in its promise of return to the Godhead, through the spread of love, the reconciling of human differences, and the placing of others ahead of the self.

Please comment on the misunderstandings between Judaism and Christianity. Is the Kaballah a valid spiritual way?

The misunderstandings are more imagined than real. The only fundamental difference of view lies in the attitude toward the Avatar who was called Jesus the Christ. The Christian community accepts that Way-shower as the true Lamb of God, in Whom God in some poorly articulated sense actually lived for the three years of the ministry prior to the crucifixion. By contrast, the Jewish religion considers Him, at most, to have been a prophet — one of a series within the Judaic tradition.

The Kaballah is a complex scheme of understanding, directed partly to interpreting hidden meanings within scriptural passages through the use of a complex numerical code. There is much occult teaching in the Kabbalistic tradition also, which goes well beyond the numerological material. Among some of the ideas we may cite one in particular, for it would be well for any seeker to contemplate the image which is made use of.

The teaching is an allegory and concerns the idea of giving, more specifically the notion of how God gives to His creatures. A man is compared to a wineglass. God holds the pitcher of abundance, and pours all wineglasses full. If the wineglass merely holds its liquid, and does not allow any out, then there is no loss, and nothing further is poured by God into the wineglass. God's gifts to the man in question simply cease. However, if the wineglass opens in itself a hole through which wine can bleed out to others, then the level in the wineglass drops, and the dropping of the level is perceived by God. Because God wishes all His wineglasses to be filled, he immediately begins to pour more from His pitcher of abundance. By this allegory, it is stated that unless a man gives out to others what he received from God — whether this be material or spiritual — then God will not exert Himself to give anything more to the man. Only by giving can we expect God to give to us.

The picture is a simple one, but it conveys a graphic image of an important truth.

What is the spiritual meaning of baptism? Why do some parts of the New Testament imply that it is a prerequisite to salvation?

The act of baptism is one which had an important part to play in the psyche of the Piscean Age. The symbolic placing of water on the head, or in some cases the immersion of the entire body in water, was capable of literally removing the build-up of negative aetheric material accumulated as a result of years of "sin", debauchery and harmful emotions. By prompting an *inner* shedding of this material at the same time as the baptism was removing the accumulation from the aetheric body, the early Baptists and others who used this rite were ensuring the most efficacious combination of purging and cleansing operations. Naturally, if

120

the convert were to sink back into the old life of debauch and negativity, the fact of having been baptised would be of no saving effect. The question of ultimate spiritual progress, as we have explained in our writings, comes down to one of *effort* on the part of the individual. No "sacrifice" by another, no amount of baptism or other ritual action, can substitute for *internal cleansing* and the expending of inner effort. Only through raising the vibrations from within can the soul ultimately succeed in reaching higher ground in a spiritual sense. However, the use of the rite of baptism was an effective way to "make the most" of the state of mind of the new convert to the church, since it removed the accumulation of a negative material that otherwise would have hindered forward progress.

Edgar Cayce predicted a horrible catastrophe that would occur before the end of the century, connected with a shift in the earth's axis. Why do the Hilarion books make no mention of this possibility?

The event in question is merely one of several possibilities regarding the "trigger" which will be used to bring the Tribulation to a close. It was known that the possibility in question had already been described in previous psychic writings, and it was desired in our books to set forth certain other mechanisms which might also be chosen to bring the "Time of Trouble" to an end. We were given the task of describing two of the alternatives: namely, the inward collapse of the earth's crust, and the passage of the earth through a "cloud" of debris, gas, etc. in space.

We must emphasize that all of these portents are merely pointing to possibilities. The future is and always has been in a great state of flux — due to man's free will. The decision as to which set of events to unleash will be made in a final way just before the circumstances are triggered, for the guides of humanity wish to preserve to themselves *all* options that may increase the effectiveness of the Tribulation upon mankind. Aside from the necessity of having the events foreshadowed in the Revelations be enacted somewhere upon the earth and be seen by at least some incarnated souls, there are no hard and fast rules which must be followed.

The person asking this question should consider the fact that many of the predictions made by Edgar Cayce did not in fact occur, and the reason why that great psychic appears to have missed the mark in certain cases. We, too, will be seen to have prophesied falsely in certain areas, when all is said and done. In our booklet, *Nations*, we have attempted to explain why this occurs, and why the true nature of prophecy is such that the *desired* result is that the dire events foreseen need not come to pass.

Please discuss cremation as opposed to burial.

The decision as to what to do with the mortal remains after the soul has fled is largely one which the individual should make. There is no particular way that is preferable from a spiritual point of view, since once the soul has departed, the fate of the body is of no more concern or impact. The only suggestion we would make is to ensure that, if cremation is chosen, a term of three full days be left between clinical death (the stopping of the heart) and the act of cremation. It takes up to three days for the astral body to detach itself completely from the physical remains. If cremation occurs before this detachment is complete, the departed consciousness will feel the flame as *intense cold*. The experience is unpleasant, and should be avoided if possible.

Please comment on Anorexia Nervosa. Why is it so widespread at the present time, and why does it seem to affect mainly young females? (This condition is marked by loss of appetite, serious drop in weight, and often an obsession with exercise).

The condition of Anorexia Nervosa is a direct result of a past life in which food was over-emphasized and illness resulted from over-eating. The previous life of gluttony would usually have caused marked obesity, and complications arising from the over-weight would normally have led to death at a relatively young age. Very often a soul learns the most by contemplating the manner and cause of its death in a life just ended, and in the case in question a very clear connection would have been made by the soul between the gluttony and the loss of the physical body through death. This would have been all the more traumatic in view of the attachment to physical pleasure which the glutton exhibits. Hence the soul would view over-eating as having a lethal aspect, and this concept would have been brought into the present life at the subconscious level.

A triggering experience is required in order to raise the subconscious memory to the conscious level. This comes about typically as a confrontation with someone who is obese and quite ill. The convergence of these two factors (illness and obesity) awakens the slumbering memory of the past gluttonous life and its untimely end, and the individual may react, or rather *over*-react, by embarking upon a drastic weight-reduction program — even where there is no obesity to begin with — often coupled with an obsession regarding exercise.

The reason why this condition is noted almost exclusively with young females is related to the access which women have to their subconscious memories, and to the emphasis which modern society places on slimness for women, particularly in advertising. It is hardly possible for a young woman to avoid the idea that a slim figure is a must, and when the triggering confrontation is encountered, the combination is sometimes enough to initiate the obsession in question.

What part might LSD and marijuana have for the spiritual unfoldment of mankind?

There is little of positive benefit available from these substances, aside from that of merely *introducing* a person to certain realms of awareness that he might not otherwise have suspected were available. The purpose for allowing these materials into the earth plane was just that: to make a person aware of other states of consciousness, in order to prompt him to look with less attachment upon the material side of existence. We speak here only of the natural euphorics and not of the distorted chemicals such as LSD. After a person has been introduced to these possibilities, he is expected to be able to pursue a course through life which will allow him to have access to such states strictly as a result of self-control, meditative techniques and a conscious seeking of the God-self within.

Is there a physical difference between men and women regarding the priesthood and the handling of the sacrements?

There is no difference of any significance in this regard. The function of the priest is to guide others in the ways of spiritual living, and men and women are equally qualified to do this. As to the handling of the sacrements, it will be evident that these materials are merely tokens of something beyond the material plane. As such, it does not matter who physically touches them.

What techniques are available for improving one's sense of self-worth?

We would like to explain three specific exercises which should have positive effects on the self-image of anyone, if pursued faithfully for a space of one month.

First, it is important to realize that negative self-pictures and feelings of worthlessness are almost always the result of negative experiences in the formative early years. Almost inevitably, the fault is with the parents of the person who has difficulty with his self-image. There is a deplorable tendency for parents to assume that the way to make a child good is to emphasize only his faults — on the mistaken assumption that making him more aware of the faults will spur him to correct them. Usually, the spur to improvement does work, but the damage done to the self-image in the process is incalculable, and can reverberate throughout the lifetime — and sometimes be carried over into the next experience in a physical body (particularly where the same parent or parents is/are encountered).

Having appreciated that the negative self-image comes from a form of "programming" which was done by others when the person was quite young, it is a relatively simple matter to set about correcting the bad effects of that programming. The first step is to determine rather precisely what programs were laid into the subconscious by the parents. In some cases, the programs relate mainly to appearance (you'll never be good-looking, you're too fat, etc.). In other cases the old tapes pertain to mental qualities (poor Esther! She just isn't too bright, you know — said within earshot of the child). These crucial thoughts become deeply implanted in the subconscious of the individual, and because he or she is not able to deal with them at the time they are first implanted, they become more and more deeply buried as time goes on. Finally, when the person reaches the late teens or early adulthood, they have sunk down so far that they are all but inaccessible. However, nothing is so deep in the subconscious that it cannot be accessed and corrected. The subconscious is like a computer. All data is available, if one knows where in the memory banks to start looking. Hence, the first step is to identify the negative thought that needs correcting.

The second step is to devise a series of counter-acting thought patterns which will negate the damaging one, and which will in effect replace the damaging concept in the subconscious. We have explained in our other writings that *repetition* is essential to the implantation of any thought permanently into the subconscious. Consider the fact that the appearance of the negative thought itself is the result of *repeated* negative statements by the parent or parent-equivalent. One must fight fire with fire.

The first exercise we suggest is to devise a two-line rhyming couplet which will state the opposite of the thought which lies at the root of the poor self-image. This may take some effort, but the result is well worth the time expended, due to the fact that the subconscious *loves a rhyme*. The subconscious memory bank will register the thought far more readily if it can be made to rhyme than if it is merely in prose form. Consider the fact that you remember still to this day the little verses of your childhood. Any reader can complete the rhyme, Hickory dickory dock..., but how many times have you heard it repeated since your childhood? Probably not at all — and yet you know the verse. Here then is the proof not only that rhyme is a great help for memorization, but also that it aids considerably in *accessing* the buried material at a much later date, long after one might have forgotten prose passages completely.

The next exercise is to assemble a list of at least twenty positive traits or qualities which you have. Do not be concerned if you are tempted to "pad" the list somewhat — the purpose is merely to read off to the subconscious a list of positive qualities so long that the subconscious gets the idea that it is endless. This raises an interesting point. The subconscious is not able to keep track of a "number" of things which is greater than about five. Of course, it can remember numbered items through association, but it is the *conscious* mind, through the trick of counting, which is able to manipulate large numbers. The subconscious cannot do this. When a list of positive qualities longer than five is read into the subconscious, it gives up counting at about 4 or 5, and after that it assigns the notion "many" to the list — not registering how long it is. There are primitive societies which even today have a counting system which goes: one, two, three, many. They have no need for counting higher than three, and have no way of doing so.

Returning to the matter at hand, it is essential to read this list to the subconscious once each day, preferably just before retiring for the night. This will give the subconscious something to chew on during the hours of sleep, as it is sorting through the experiences of the day.

It is also best to actually "feel good" about each of the points in the list. Try to develop a feeling of satisfaction regarding each of the points as they come up. After a week or two, this procedure will automatically produce the sense of satisfaction.

It does not matter what is on the list. The points can relate to appearance, to mental qualities, to kindness, musical gifts, athletic skill or whatever. The only requisite is that they be desirable qualities of which one can be proud.

Now we are not advising pride as an antidote. However, because the idea of self-pride is the converse of the feeling of unworthiness, even though both represent a lopsided attitude, it is helpful to try to push oneself in the direction of the other extreme for the duration of the exercise we are suggesting, on the understanding that, later, a balanced middle road between the two can be sought.

The last exercise in the triad program is strictly a physical one. It consists of two parts: sit-ups and vertical bouncing. We have discussed the benefits of sit-ups in other writings, mainly their good effect on the solar plexus chakra and hence on the entire physical vehicle. However, we have not yet stressed the positive results which arise from the act of moving the body rhythmatically up and down while in a standing posture. There are currently available certain devices constructed like miniature trampolines, on which the user can bounce while standing. The devices are extremely beneficial from several standpoints: Firstly, the exercise of vertical bouncing stresses the muscles of the legs and abdomen in a regular and non-traumatic way. Secondly, the backbone is subjected to a variation from zero gravity to about two times normal gravity. This alternately compresses and expands the spine, thus working the discs and ligaments of this crucial part of the body. Next, the exercise stimulates the lymph system into discharging its load of waste material more quickly than normal. It is mainly for this reason that, at first, the exerciser may feel somewhat light-headed after only a minute or so of bouncing. Those whose lymph systems are relatively clear will not have this experience. Finally, the bouncing exercise causes the body to move rhythmically up and down through the earth's magnetic field. Since the body — and particularly the nervous system — is an electrical conductor, the fact of causing this conductor to "cut through" the earth's magnetic field will result in a mild alternating current throughout the system, at a low frequency (the same as that of the bouncing). This phenomenon brings about a stimulation of the nervous system, and essentially a calming of the entire system. It acts as a lulling repetition which unties knotted regions of the nervous pathways, and has a rebound effect up into the aetheric body as well.

While this part of the program may not seem particularly aimed at improving the self image, it actually would have a very pronounced effect on the self-worth feelings, due to the fact that the state of the physical body would be so dramatically improved. It is generally true that, at a certain level of the subconscious, the picture of the self is intimately bound up with the state of the physical body. Indeed, the first concept which anyone has of the self is based on the body. Identification with the physical form is that which allows a young baby to begin to form its image of itself. Hence, if that primordial token of the self — the body — can be brought into the healthiest and most vigorous state (which would be largely accomplished by this exercise program, barring inherent weakness or advanced age), it follows that the self-image too could not help but be improved.

Please comment on the Lord's Prayer.

This prayer needs little comment from any spiritual source. Its power to save and protect individuals is immense, partly because of the One from Whom it came, and partly because of certain mantric qualities which it contains. Let us say simply that no other prayer is as effective for protection in the face of evil as this beautiful teaching from the lips of the Master.

Could you please unravel something of the mystery of Stonehenge?

This arrangement of ancient rocks has remained a mystery ever since its rediscovery in the more recent past. Many attempts have been made to decode the meaning of the geometry of the stones, but no interpreter has yet realised the most important significance of Stonehenge: namely that it is a focal point through which energies from a different plane — one could say a different universe — are able to enter the earth realm.

The specific emplacement of the stones allows a particular contact between the planes to be established, and it is through this contact that many of the finest virtues of the English race have been implanted and fostered. Without Stonehenge, England could not have developed the sense of fair play and honour which she has bequeathed to the rest of the world, nor could she have displayed the delightful "understated" sense of humor for which the British race is famous. Other fine qualities also belong to the "package" of traits which have been nurtured through the vibrations which have flooded England from the magical focus of Stonehenge, but we have described the ones which have been most important in terms of advancing the spirituality and nobility of the race of man.

Please discuss giving and receiving, and how this concept and balancing it affects our endeavors.

The gift which God has bestowed upon the human soul is that of eternal, focused consciousness. But He meant man also to know the joy of giving to others, even as He knew the Divine Joy of giving eternity to His earth children. Therefore, He arranged for man to have *more* than the essentials for the support of life, so that there would be extra to be given to those who are in need, or to those who are dependent upon the giver for support. In giving to others, man approaches closer to his own divinity for it is the nature of the Godhead to shower gifts and abundance upon all of the creatures that have emanated from Him. Through giving, and through creativeness, man rises to take his place among the noble races of the cosmos.

Yet there is one more aspect to this question which we wish to discuss. There are those who, because of self-worth or self-image problems, will not allow others to give to *them*. All readers will know certain individuals who steadfastly discourage others from giving them gifts, and who make the giver feel he has somehow done something wrong in offering the gift. This attitude is unfortunate, for the one discouraging the giver is refusing to allow that other soul to experience the act of giving — the joy of bestowing something upon another. The person who thus discourages others from giving is refusing to give the *gift of giving!* For here, too, is a gift to another: *allowing that other person also to know the joy of giving.*

We would say, then, that he who truly aspires to spiritual progress not only gives freely to others, but also allows others to give to him, accepting graciously that which is offered. For indeed, do not those gifts from others come ultimately from God? And is it right to refuse God the joy of giving?

What effect has the act of "calling forth the judgement"

on entities, as is practiced by the Summit Lighthouse?

This practise is extremely effective, if done by one who has the requisite authority. We are not allowed to comment further on this question however, as the concept has been given through another channel.

What can be done for mentally or emotionally disturbed people who have become addicted to psychotropic drugs? Withdrawal from the drugs seems merely to make them worse, while continuing simply entrenches feelings of helplessness and anger.

The answer here also applies to any addiction to any substance. We include coffee, smoking, alcohol and even the eating of particular and harmful materials. The best solution that we can possibly recommend is to call upon higher forces to come to one's aid. The help is most certainly available; it is merely a matter of summoning that help to one's side.

Now, the conceptual framework within which the help is called depends greatly on the mental categories, the background and the expectations of the person concerned.

It is well known that many former drunkards and alcoholics have been cured literally overnight by being "converted" to Christ's message. There are numerous testimonials by such people as to how, on the night when Christ entered their hearts, they stopped needing or wanting to drink. Now this process — the very fundamental one of embracing the Christ and expecting help — is extremely effective. Its effect comes from the fact that the Christ principle does in fact literally enter the bodies of the former addict and remove the distortions which had previously driven the person to the bottle. From that point on, provided the new convert continues to strengthen and improve his own spirituality (even along conventional religious lines) the cure will often remain and become permanent.

This type of "cure" is best for those whose background is of a conventional nature, and who have neither the interest nor inclination for extending their understanding of occult or spiritual matters beyond that level. Indeed, many are caught in the notion that everything spiritual or occult is evil or weird in some way, and they instinctively shy away from it.

The other level is one at which the sufferer does have a basic grasp of the spiritual realities which surround him, and understands that many levels exist from which specific entities can be called down to help with a problem of addiction. In this case, it is simply a matter of calling upon God's angels to come to one's aid. There is a pact that has been made between the angels and mankind, by which whenever any human calls upon an angel for help, one must come. Those who see clairvoyantly can testify to the truth of this statement, simply by requesting an angel to show himself.

Of course, the summoning of the Christ principle would also work for one whose spiritual understanding is more opened. We are merely trying to sketch the possibilities that are most likely to appeal to different understandings.

In short, what we are saying is that the best procedure to combat any kind of addiction is to ask for help from higher levels. The perception of these higher levels, however, depends upon the mentality and understanding of the one who is calling for the aid.

Can you comment on homeopathic remedies in general, and on the Bach Flower Remedies in particular?

The nature of the homeopathic response to illness and disease is a unique one. It seeks to combat illness through the administration of small quantities of a substance which, if taken in large dosages by a healthy individual, would produce the very symptoms which characterize that illness. Little is understood about the mechanism by which the homeopathic remedies have their effect. The secret is simple to understand, however, when it is realized that the homeopathic materials function not at the physical level, but at the aetheric level. Because they operate aetherically — and primarily on the aetheric body — and because reactions at the aetheric level are in general the reverse of those at the physical level, the aetheric counterpart of the administered homeopathic remedy acts as a *cure* for the aetheric body, the latter eventually transmitting the improvement to the physical form.

In regard to the Bach Remedies, we should mention first of all that the discoverer and developer of these potions was a very advanced soul from a lofty plane, who volunteered to come to the earth in order to give this concept to the human race. His writings, and particularly his beautiful book, *Heal Thyself,* should be read and carefully meditated on by all Workers of the Light. In no other booklet now extant is there contained such a precise and beautiful explanation of the reason for diseases of all kinds.

As to the nature of the Bach Remedies themselves, it will be clear to all those who have tried them that in many cases there is great help available from these liquids. The efficacy arises again at the aetheric level, but in a special process. The Bach Remedies act first and foremost on the mental body, which is not identical with the aetheric (though they are strongly inter-connected). The Remedies thus have a powerful influence on the general mental attitudes, and it is for this reason that they are used so extensively to correct "mental body" flaws such as cowardice, fear, loss of hope, and the like. However, there are also many diseases which afflict the physical body and which have their origin in some lopsidedness at the mental plane level. These afflictions can therefore be alleviated through the Remedies, which act first to correct the mental body, and then the physical body.

Is the abnormally high suicide rate in Seattle the result of the excessively cloudy and wet weather in that city?

The suicide rate is partly due to the oppressive nature of the weather patterns of that city, but there is another side to the story. Indeed, those who are drawn to Seattle as a birthplace are in many cases souls who have yielded to the temptation of suicide in past lives, and now must again be put through the temptation — in the hope that they will prove stronger this time. Here is an opportunity for us to explain the true nature of suicide, and the karmic consequences which it brings in its wake. Suicide is almost never a positive act. Almost without exception it is an act of desperation, resorted to by one who wishes merely to end the pain of life. In most cases, the person attempting to take his own life does not understand the spiritual realities surrounding his earthly existence, else he would not allow such a temptation to sway him. For the truth of the matter is simply that anyone who attempts or succeeds in committing suicide must inevitably be presented with similar circumstances in a later phase of his earth experience, with the proviso that the test must be a little bit *harder* the next time. Thus, not only is the person not solving his problem through suicide, but he is guaranteeing that he will have to go through the same pain again which he tried to end before, and that the choice against self-destruction will be even harder to make. This notion should give serious pause to any contemplating the ending of their physical lives.

Now, since a previous suicide must inevitably be drawn back into incarnation at a location and in a life-pattern which will again present him with the choice of self-destruction, it can be understood that, with its oppressive and gloomy weather, Seattle is an ideal location for enacting the drama this time around. Indeed, in a large portion of Seattle's population there is at least a distant history of self-destruction in past lives, even though most have more recently passsed the same test as once they failed. However, because the germ of self-destruction is still faintly alive within them, they have been drawn back to that city for an incarnation in order to give themselves the opportunity to transmute that negative fragment into something positive — for by living most of an incarnation under an oppressive weather pattern, such persons are able to develop an attitude of acceptance and insularity which allows them to withstand the pressures which the depressing weather exerts.

It is more complicated than that. Such persons — those who have turned themselves around, so to speak — are able to pass along a certain suicidal tendency genetically to their children. This then makes them ideal parents for a soul who has recently failed the suicide test, and has taken his own life: firstly the parents pass along the genetic imperfection which prompts the depressive attitude that leads often to thoughts of suicide, but *secondly* the parents are ones who have *passed* that same test themselves, and thus can show the new soul, by example and by teaching, how one goes about resisting the negative pressures of a suicidal tendency.

Please explain the symbolic meaning of the zero ("0") in a house number, etc.

The zero is a relative newcomer to the world of mathematical reckoning. The principal digits from 1 to 9 are the main significators for humanity in its present phase. However, when it does appear that a person is being "chased around" by zeros with a non-statistical frequency, then the meaning is to be sought in the notion that zero means the "absence" of something. Look for the idea that something is "missing" in the life pattern, or in the emotional or mental nature. A careful scrutiny will in every case explain fully why the guides have selected the zero to pass symbolic information to the individual.

Was Jehovah a space ship commander acting without the approval of the Galactic Confederation?

The name Jehovah was indeed that given by early men to an entity who "came down from the sky" to be among them. However, the matter is too complex to explain fully in this newsletter. The concepts currently available to this channel are not sufficient to allow us to do justice to the question.

Note from the Editor:

For this issue of Lightline — the last published issue — we have not asked specific questions of Hilarion. Mr. Cooke was directed merely to open the channel as he does for the books, and to take down whatever is given. The result of that session follows.

Those of you who have sent in questions that have not yet been answered may feel disappointed that we are not making an effort to 'tidy up' all those remaining. In actual fact the Lightline readership has been very forthcoming with questions, and even now we are sitting on more than enough of them to fill many Lightlines. Perhaps, in some way, Hilarion knows the questions that have been posed. Or let us rather say — perhaps he can discern what the really important topics are that still remain to be dealt with. In the material that follows, he has sought to bring out the essence of the spiritual path, and to lay down — perhaps for the last time in this form — the thoughts, actions and attitudes which those on the Path should hold ever before their inner consciousness. We hope you will find this transmission as informative and uplifting as we did.

This last issue of Lightline is one in which we wish to set out as clearly as possible the precepts that should govern enlightened souls while in incarnation, and the basic goals of a life on this planet. In addition, we will attempt to explain the reasons behind the preparation of the series of books which bear the name Hilarion. We think that after the reader has digested what we will now explain, he will perceive with a broader insight the Path on which his feet are set, and the perilous journey which all souls must make in the months and years ahead.

The Trial Ahead

We have spoken of a perilous journey, and we stress that, *even for those on the Path*, it will be a time of testing, of temptation, of fear. There will be periods when it seems that the guides and guardians have deserted you, that the truths and principles you have been learning no longer function, that the desperate plight of the world has no hope of rescue.

It will be a time when all of the lights of the spirit will seem to go out at once.

The purpose of the testing phase shortly to be initiated is simple to state: it is to truly distinguish the evolved souls from those who do not wish to see the truth; it is to make certain that the ones who enter into the New Age of peace, light and love are those who can truly be counted on to work for the spiritual progress of *all* their brothers — and to whom matters of the self have faded into unimportance.

All along it has been known — at least by the minority of souls able to read aright the message of scriptures — that when the time of the end would come, it would come like a snare, a trap suddenly sprung upon the world, catching unawares the souls who had not prepared for the worst. Throughout the scriptures this message is given over and over.

It is not our purpose here to describe again the events soon to befall the earth. That message has already been given — not only in our books, but in many, many other writings over the past 2000 years. If wayward mankind can still turn a deaf ear to these warnings, then little good would be served by again ringing the changes of catastrophe and upheaval which the future holds.

Better by far to use this space to explain the broader perspective on what is happening to this planet, and to give to the earnest seeker the tools, the understanding, to allow him to pass through the testing period unscathed.

Let us begin by talking of light: not merely the light which is seen by the eyes as the visible spectrum, but the true meaning of light at the symbolic level. Light is, in the final analysis, that which ensouls all that lives — *on any level of being.* The light which humanity was intended finally to seek is the *light within:* the "Light which lighteth every man into the world." And that light is the light of the soul, as far as mankind is concerned.

Yet man has sought only the brightness outside himself, for the greater part of his history on this planet. He has followed the glitter of gold, the flash of tinsel and pomp, the marquee lights of fame and renown. Always he has turned outside of himself for the answers to his existence riddle: in times of strong religious waves on the planet, he has turned to an organized church; in times of apostacy and doubt, he has made science the totem of truth and the standard by which to accept or reject an idea; in times of superstition and fear, he has sought the protection of shamans, amulets and blood sacrifice. But only a handful of men — and only at long intervals — have perceived that the light of truth, the light of the Universe, the Light of God... lay *within* their own beings. Only these few have realized that *they* were the only true custodians of God's essence: the Light that lighteth every man into the world. And only they have made the great leap forward into the higher realms of love and truth, thus escaping from the wheel of rebirth.

But now, what was reserved for the few must become the watchword of many millions of human souls. At last the gates of enlightenment can swing wide open, for at last there are enough souls incarnate *together* upon the earth to take up and receive this light, without becoming blinded and disoriented by the immense brightening of the spirit which is about to happen.

We have come upon a key idea here, and we wish to ensure that its import is properly grasped. In ages past, when darkness held sway on the earth and men were unifomly selfish and blinded by the lure of the material world, any flooding of the earth with light from higher realms *would have meant the disappearance of man as a physical life-form on this planet*. We say this in all sincerity, for the truth is that such higher vibrations would have been lethal for the souls then in the vast majority on the earth. In order to allow light to enter the earth in a *safe* manner, there must be human receptacles where it can reside. Otherwise, the light would simply blind those who tried to understand it. Lacking any grasp of spiritual reality, such benighted souls would have misperceived the new energy, and would have twisted it into an excuse to become even more worldly, or more cruel, or more animalistic. The result would have been racial self-annihilation.

We cannot stress this point too strongly, for a proper grasp of its significance will allow the seeker to understand the nature of the events which he sees all around him on the earth, as the old age crumbles away. Think of it in these terms: it is clear that the New Age energies are waxing; this is evidenced by the upsurge of interest in all things occult, the increase in vegetarianism, the trend toward greater bodily purity and health (jogging, the anti-smoking movement, etc.), and other phenomena. These positive manifestations are due to the fact that there were souls on the earth capable of receiving the new energies and transmuting them into positive and helpful ideas. But at the same time on the earth there are degenerate souls who think of nothing but themselves and the worldly goals of wealth, fame or temporal power. It is these souls who have used the new energies in a negative way, fomenting hatred and warfare, practising torture, leading rebellions, terrorist attacks and coups against established governments. If the world held only souls of such low vibration, then the flooding in of the new light and energy would simply be used for destruction and the race itself would be imperiled.

It is for this reason that the doors of light could not be flung wide until there were enough seekers in incarnation to be able to receive and keep pure the light of truth which is to stand at the core of the New Age. These guardians of spiritual truth had to be in place before the tap could be turned on, so to speak. And it is upon their efforts and dedication that the success of this last great gamble will rest.

For it is indeed a gamble. It is known full well that many souls will refuse to turn toward the light of spiritual understanding. It is known full well that even the 'decent' souls — the ones who abide by noble principles but who have never cared to expand their focus of understanding to encompass loftier concepts of truth — will be terribly bewildered and frightened by the events soon to befall this planet; so much so that they may turn away from their God, believing that He has abandoned them in a hostile universe, or worse, that He does not even exist. And it is known that even the seekers — you to whom this newsletter is addressed — may fall into despair at the havoc you see around you, to the point where you may not exert yourself to save your brothers.

Indeed, that last risk represents the greatest gamble of all. Those already of base vibration are unlikely to be jolted out of their spiritual lethargy through witnessing destruction which they themselves have largely caused. *But the basically 'good' or 'decent' souls we have mentioned will be crying out for help from anyone who can explain the circumstances into which the earth has fallen, and many of these will be literally snatched from the jaws of destruction by the efforts of those whose feet are securely on the Path.* (By destruction, we mean separation from the more noble fraction of humanity, and the loss of individual

140

personality as the soul is returned to the spiritual melting pot from which all life-streams are originally breathed forth. For a deeper explanation of this concept, the reader is referred to our book, *Other Kingdoms.*)

Speaking the truth when asked.

We cannot stress too greatly to the seeker the importance of *stating the truth as he perceives it to be,* and not watering it down to suit the presumed prejudices of the questioner. The time for gentle answers has all but passed. When the events begin to take place, the questions will be asked in earnest, and — perhaps for the first and only time in a long series of incarnations — the confused or frightened soul will be open to receiving the light of the spirit.

We wish to dwell further on this point, lest it not be fully appreciated. We have said in our earlier writings that the replies to those seeking answers of a spiritual nature should be tailored to the understanding of the person seeking the information. While that advice has been valid for the initial period of trial — since most questions from non-seekers are prompted by curiosity alone — it will not do for the last and most desperate phase of the test. During the latter times, those who come to seekers for help will be driven to it by fear or confusion, and they will be fully open to whatever light is shed by the answer they receive. Many such souls will be required to make great spiritual strides in a very short time, and the result will be considerable stress on their physical and other bodies. This will be paralleled for many of them by a radical change in diet, as certain foodstuffs on which they had become dependent suddenly become scarce or unavailable. But it cannot be any other way. There has been ample time for all souls to find the key to the light of truth, for it has been told to man in countless ways in countless lands, stretching back over the entire period during which he has used this planet as a base for incarnation. There is no longer any time left to allow the stragglers and the laggards to have their way. If they cannot voluntarily turn from the lure of worldly goals, then these things must be snatched away, to leave them nothing but their own inner strength for support. And very soon it will be time for that final test to be run.

We know that these sound like hard words. But the times that are coming are equally hard, and you who know the truth will be required to speak it unhesitatingly for your brothers. All the higher beings who care for humanity's struggle can do nothing without your willing help. The law says that we cannot directly interfere with conscious thought on the earth plane. We cannot force our understanding on those not open to it (nor would we wish to do so), and we are prohibited from taking a direct hand in the dissemination of spiritual truth aside from initiating certain writings as we have done. But even that contribution has required the willing help of our human channel, as well as the many others who have come together with him to help disseminate these works. Without that participation our thoughts and words would have reached no one.

Thus it is upon *your* shoulders that the salvation of the race rests. Your guides and helpers from higher planes are counting upon you to do your utmost as and when the opportunities present themselves — always remembering that light is to be given only when requested. You are not expected to go out into the street and prosyletize converts to this or any particular way of thinking. Know that those whom you can best help will be brought across your path by their own guides, and know that if one of your brothers comes to you for help, his guides are confident that you are *able* to give him just the help he requires. Here we have another great truth which all seekers would do well to bear in mind. Let us expand upon this thought for a short space.

Each human being has something to offer his brothers. Each soul can learn *something* from every other soul. But when it comes to offering *spiritual* help, the guides know who is best suited to aid any given soul in need. Moreover they are perfectly capable of bringing the soul in their

142

charge into contact with any other soul on the earth plane, provided physical location is not a problem. Thus, be assured that whenever anyone comes to you for help, *it is because you have the means of helping that person.* Do not doubt the wisdom of the guides who have arranged the meeting; simply seek the answer, the key, that will unlock the problem which your brother presents to you. If you ask for help from your own guides, it will be given.

Again, we stress the main point: keep yourself centered amid the chaos that will be seen to swirl around you, and do not hesitate to reach out in aid to any who seek your help. For this is the crucial point of the entire trial. The earlier phases of this test have afflicted primarily the less advanced areas of the world — countries like Cambodia have been almost erased from the surface of the globe; others like Poland have slipped deeper into slavery as a result of their own efforts to escape it. As yet no paramount test has been applied to the more advanced regions such as North America. But we have stated elsewhere that *the human family is one,* and that the events that afflict one part of the life-stream must eventually have repercussions on all parts. Soon those repercussions will be in evidence. And with them comes the 'secret weapon' of humanity's guides: the hoped-for willingness of the world's seekers to stand forth and help their brothers to a broader and nobler understanding of existence and its goals. For until the troubles clearly beset the more advanced areas of the world (where the great majority of seekers resides), this last phase of 'salvation from within' cannot be run. The average citizen of Canada and the United States, for example, has little interest in the esoteric truths of existence on this planet, and could scarcely be expected to listen to someone up on a soapbox warning him that the end of the present civilization is at hand. Not until he sees the stark evidence of that ending will he seek help and reassurance, and not until then can he be aided.

This, we hope, places into proper perspective the scenario of upheaval that will soon be initiated.

Can the future be changed?

Perhaps a word is in order to explain why we have, earlier in our writings through this channel, suggested that much was in flux in regard to the outcome of the present impasse on the earth. On many occasions we have seemed to avoid direct questions about the future chaos, by pointing out that man had free will and could use it to soften greatly the blow of the Tribulation hammer. While these statements were indeed correct, and while humanity *could* have snatched itself out of the path of the juggernaut now bearing down upon it, it has all along been clear from this level that it would take a substantial cataclysm to 'get through' to those souls who have hardened themselves against the words of truth over many lives, and that there would be a vast number of human souls that would not even care to regenerate the baseness within them. In the past we have spoken as if that fraction of 'lost souls' might become quite small with the onset of the difficulties, as individuals were driven to seek a nobler path by the chaos around them. Again there *was* that possibility. No being at any level of awareness can possibly say for sure that such-and-such a soul will not make it into the new vibration. But, alas, while individuals can, through effort, attain *any* level of regeneration in a relatively short time, the truth is that only a small fraction of the baser sector of the human family is likely to make those efforts. It is estimated that fully half of the human life-stream must be cut away in the great tragedy that mankind is about to perpetrate upon itself. The fraction could even be greater.
These are hard words. But the time for softness, for 'making allowances', has passed. We hope that the reader will not be appalled at the forthrightness with which we are making these statements. From our perspective, the timing is so close that human free will can now play only a minor role in modifying the events. And since much that was in flux is now relatively fixed, the true dimensions of

humanity's predicament can now be told.

Around the world there are seekers of many stamps. There are those who follow gurus and are caught up mainly in the notion of self-improvement or self-purification. There are others who know that much destruction has been foreshadowed in prophetic writings, but who hope that by 'thinking positively' they can avert the worst that the prophets have foreseen. There are others who have become trapped in false doctrines, following leaders or ideas that can only sidetrack their energies and prevent them from being of true service to their brothers in the great time of need that soon will come.

To all of these potential torches of spiritual truth we send out a call. *Leave your preoccupation with self! Take up the cross of service — even as Christ Himself did — and reach out to your confused and frightened brothers. For now is the darkest hour that humanity has ever faced. If you cannot find within yourself the strength, the wisdom and the love to care for the lost sheep among you, then the experiment which humanity represents is doomed to failure.*

Update

The above message was transmitted several years ago, at a point in time when the prospects appeared to us extremely bleak. We wished to sound a clear warning about the distinct possibilities of upheaval, which were then only months from manifestation.

However this realm of earth is very dear to the heart of the Creator, and for the sake of the millions who love Him, He stretched out His mighty hand to shield the billions who do not. This was done by channelling divine energy through the Seekers of the world. Though they represent a mere handful compared to the vast population of this planet, their purity of dedication and their love for their brothers were great enough to accept and channel that immense inrush of light. They knew it not, but their commitment to spirit saved the earth.

Matters still hang in the balance, in terms of the stability of your civilization. The reprieve continues, but there remains always the great risk that one act of insanity on the part of man could bring this phase of history abruptly to a close.

Whether or not this occurs, know that all of you who have made a commitment to the ideals of the New Age of brotherhood and peace will find yourselves in positions from which you can help others in their time of need. Know, too, that the period of upheaval will be of relatively short duration. Hold fast to your beliefs through the night of chaos, for the most glorious of dawns awaits your dazzled eyes when the darkness lifts.

The earth is destined to become what all of you long for in your hearts: a garden of joy, where tears are shed only for happiness, and the laughter of His children echos to the farthest galaxy.

May the peace and blessing of all the higher beings who care for humanity's struggle be with you forevermore.

OM MANI PADME HUM

Hilarion Mailing List

If you wish to be kept informed regarding Workshops in the Hilarion material, speaking tours by Maurice B. Cooke, and our regular special offers of new books and cassette tapes at reduced prices, please write to us at the address below and we will be happy to include your name on our regular mailing list.

Marcus Books
195 Randolph Rd.,
Toronto, Canada, M4G 3S6